Editor

Brent L. Fox, M. Ed.

Editor in Chief

Karen J. Goldfluss, M.S. Ed.

Creative Director

Sarah M. Fournier

Cover Artist

Diem Pascarella

Art Coordinator

Renée Mc Elwee

Illustrator

Mark Mason

Imaging

Amanda R. Harter

Publisher

Mary D. Smith, M.S. Ed.

GRADE 4

TCR 3657

INSTANT READING COMPREHENSION PRACTICE

- Provides 240 fiction and nonfiction quick-read activities for applying eight comprehension strategies

- Reinforces reading skills throughout the year

- Includes a "Strategies in Writing" section to practice comprehension skills in an open-ended, short-answer format

- **Correlated to Common Core State Standards**

This is a **tapsponder** enabled resource!

Teacher Created Resources

D0898497

Authors

Ruth Foster, M. Ed.

Mary S. Jones, M. Ed.

CORRELATED TO **COMMON CORE** STANDARDS

For correlations to the Common Core State Standards, see pages 141–142. Correlations can also be found at *http://www.teachercreated.com/standards.*

Teacher Created Resources

6421 Industry Way
Westminster, CA 92683
www.teachercreated.com

ISBN: 978-1-4206-3657-4

© *2015 Teacher Created Resources*
Made in U.S.A.

Teacher Created Resources

Table of Contents

Introduction

Instant Reading Comprehension Practice provides short reading and writing exercises that develop and strengthen the skills needed for reading comprehension.

This book is divided into two main sections: *Comprehension Activities* and *Strategies in Writing*. *Comprehension Activities* is divided into eight sub-sections that focus specifically on each of the following comprehension skills:

- Finding Main Ideas
- Noting Details
- Using Context Clues
- Identifying Facts and Opinions

- Finding Cause and Effect
- Sequencing
- Making Inferences
- Predicting Outcomes

Each sub-section includes at least 30 passages with questions designed to challenge students and guide them towards mastery in one of the eight skill areas.

The *Strategies in Writing* section provides students with the opportunity to identify and practice the same comprehension skills but in an open-ended, short-answer format. The activities in this section allow students to focus on a specific strategy and to think more critically as they respond to a given writing task.

A teacher can

- choose to focus on one skill exclusively, going sequentially through the exercises.
- do a few exercises from each skill set to provide daily variety.
- assign specific exercises that will introduce, match, and/or strengthen strategies covered in the classroom.

Writing activities can be assigned at any time and in any order, but each activity focuses on a particular strategy. The strategy is noted at the top of the page. Each strategy has four activity pages, except for *Making Inferences* and *Predicting Outcomes*, which have three each.

Teaching Tips for Specific Exercises

You may want to go through one or two exercises together with the class.

At first, focus on critical-thinking skills rather than speed. Fluency and rate of reading will improve as students practice and gain confidence with each targeted skill.

Remind students that they should read EVERY answer choice. The first answer may sound correct, but there might be a better choice. If they can cross out just one wrong answer, they will have a much better chance of choosing the correct answer.

Finding Main Ideas

Students may find it helpful to sum up what they just read in a short sentence or two before reading the answer choices. Other students may find it helpful to first make a list of three or four key words from the text. Both strategies can help students focus on the most important parts of a passage and not be mislead by incorrect answer choices.

Remind students to choose an answer that covers most of whom or what the paragraph is about. Usually, wrong answers will focus either on details that are too small or too broad. For example, you may read a paragraph about three interesting things to see in California. Facts are given about the Golden Gate Bridge, a tree called Methuselah that is over 4,800 years old, and migrating gray whales off the coast. An answer that *only* talks about Methuselah is too "small" because it leaves out the bridge and the whales. An answer that talks about *all* the interesting things to see in California is too "big." The main idea is three interesting things from California, not *every* interesting thing. In other words, you should be thinking, "Not too big, not too small, but just right!"

Pick the correct answer. Students should think about what answer is too big, too small, just right . . . or just wrong!

The archer fish swims just under the surface of the water. When it spots a bug or spider hanging over the water from a twig or leaf, the archer fish spits! The archer fish spits so hard that it knocks the bug into the water and then gobbles it up!

What is the main idea?

A. Archer fish swim under the surface of the water when looking for food. (too small)

B. Different kinds of fish eat different kinds of food. (too big)

C. Archer fish have an unusual strategy for capturing food. (just right)

Noting Details

Remind students not to panic if they read a passage with a lot of details. They do not have to memorize or remember all the facts and figures! They can always go back and check the passage. Read the following example:

> Most of Earth is covered by oceans. The largest ocean is the Pacific Ocean. The second-largest ocean is the Atlantic Ocean. The third-largest ocean is the Indian Ocean.
>
> What is the second-largest ocean?
> **A.** Pacific Ocean
> **B.** Atlantic Ocean
> **C.** Indian Ocean
> *Answer: B*

Ask students if they had to memorize what they read to answer the question or if they went back and looked it up. Point out that all the information they need is still right in front of them and can be reread as many times as necessary.

Using Context Clues

Remind students not to stop reading! Reassure students that they are not expected to know what a word means or what word should go in the blank. They are solving a puzzle! They **must** finish reading the prompt. Then, they can reread the sentence while inserting one of the answer choices into the blank. Usually, they can eliminate choices because some answers will not make sense.

For example, no one expects a child to know the word *discombobulated* (confused, frustrated). Yet students can correctly choose it if they use the process of elimination, as seen in the following example:

> Jonah was _____ by all the bright lights, loud noises, and people rushing by.
>
> What word best completes the sentence?
> **A.** taught
> **B.** discombobulated
> **C.** lifted
> *Answer: B*

Point out that even if students couldn't understand the word *discombobulated*, they could cross out and eliminate *taught* and *lifted*. They could still get the right answer!

Identifying Facts and Opinions

Have students ask themselves, "Is this something I think, or do I know for certain?"

> *Riding a bike is more fun than roller-skating.* If I **think** it, it is an **opinion**.

> *Some people like to ride bikes more than they like to roller-skate.* If it is **certain** or if I can prove it, it is a **fact**.

Finding Cause and Effect

Have students ask themselves, "What happened, and why did it happen?"

What happened is the **effect**. **Why** it happened is the **cause**. If they forget this, students can write **What** = **Effect** and **Why** = **Cause** on the top of their page until the information can easily be recalled.

Example: When Lisa read the book, she learned that a giraffe's heart is two feet long.

What happened? (**effect**) Lisa learned something. Why did it happen? (**cause**) Lisa read a book.

Sequencing

Ask students to read over the sentences in the order they think the events happened. Think about what comes first and what comes later. Think about whether the order makes sense. Make sure the last sentence could not have happened until the previous ones did. Consider the following example:

> 1. When her television turned on, Ms. Larson thought Scott was a genius.
>
> 2. Ms. Larson's television set wasn't working.
>
> 3. Ms. Larson didn't see Scott plug the cord into the electrical socket.
>
> What is the correct sequence?
>   A. 1, 2, 3
>   B. 3, 2, 1
>   C. 2, 3, 1   *Answer: C*

Making Inferences

When we make an inference, we use **clues** from the story to figure out something the author hasn't told us.

Example: Caesar's heart pounded! He felt a cold trickle of sweat run down his back.

Most likely, was Caesar hungry, tired, or afraid? If Caesar was hungry, he probably wouldn't be having such a strong physiological reaction. The same logic can be applied to being tired. Being afraid is the only logical answer.

Predicting Outcomes

When we predict an outcome, we make a logical guess about what is going to happen next. Remind students not to answer what happened. They should only be concerned about what might happen in the **future**.

Example: At the beach, Callie saw a sign that said, "No swimming. Dangerous currents."

Have students make logical guesses about what might happen next. (Callie stays out of the water; Callie goes into the water, and she gets caught in a dangerous current, etc.)

Remember: Insist that students read every answer choice! Have them eliminate or cross out the answer choices that don't make sense or that they know are wrong!

Name _____ **Date** _____

Be Careful What You Wish For

Bo's family moved from a small house into a much larger house. "Every room in the new house is bigger," said Bo's mom. Bo was excited to have a much bigger bedroom. Bo's chores in the new house included cleaning his room and sweeping the kitchen. After living in the new house for a month, Bo started wishing he still had his old room. It had a lot less space to clean!

What is the main idea?

A. Bo was glad to have a bigger room until he realized it would need more cleaning.

B. Bo did not want a bigger room because he preferred his old room.

C. Bo was happy to be getting a bigger room because there would be a lot more space for him and his brother to share.

Surprising Visit

Rose and her parents were invited for lunch at Rose's aunt and uncle's house. Rose didn't want to go because she wanted to spend the afternoon with her friends instead. When she walked into the house, only her aunt and uncle were there. Rose immediately knew she'd be bored. Suddenly, all her friends jumped out from behind the furniture. "Surprise!" they shouted. "Happy birthday!"

What is the main idea?

A. Rose knew she would be bored at her aunt and uncle's house.

B. Rose's friends gave her a surprise birthday party at her aunt and uncle's house.

C. It was Rose's parents' idea to surprise her at her aunt and uncle's house.

A Day for Dad

It was the night before Father's Day when Jack realized that he hadn't yet bought a gift for his dad. As he lay in bed, Jack thought of an idea. The next morning, Jack was the first to wake up. He cleaned his room, made his dad's favorite breakfast, and washed all the dishes. When Jack's dad awoke and saw what was done, he said it was the best Father's Day present ever.

What is the main idea?

A. Jack woke up early because he realized he forgot to do his chores.

B. Jack's dad looks forward to Father's Day because he likes to get presents.

C. On Father's Day, Jack did something nice for his dad instead of buying him a gift.

Night Talking

Jason has an unusual habit. For a while, he didn't even know he had it. Jason's brother Evan is the only one who knows about it. Every night, Jason talks in his sleep. Evan hears him from across the room. One night, Jason talked in his sleep about a forest ranger trying to steal his lunch! Evan recorded Jason talking in his sleep and then played the recording for him the following morning. That's when Jason found out about his unusual habit.

What is the main idea?

A. Jason didn't know that he talks in his sleep until he heard a recording of it.

B. Evan used to throw pillows across the room to get Jason to stop talking in his sleep.

C. Jason pretended to talk in his sleep to try to trick Evan.

Name _____ **Date** _____

Dress-Up Drama

Sue's mom left her jewelry near the kitchen sink while washing the dishes. Without asking, Sue used her mom's jewelry to play dress-up. Sue put all her dress-up stuff away when it was time to clean up. The next morning, Sue remembered that she still needed to return the jewelry. She looked through her box of dress-up clothes and couldn't find her mother's jewelry anywhere. How was she going to explain this to her mom?

What is the main idea?

A. Sue's mom allowed Sue to use the jewelry for playing dress-up.

B. Sue put all of the dress-up clothes away when it was time to clean up.

C. Sue used her mother's jewelry without asking and then lost it.

Island Living

St. Kilda is a tiny chain of Scottish islands formed from the rim of an ancient volcano. The islands are located more than 40 miles from the nearest land. Steep cliffs, strong winds, and high tides make visits to the island a difficult undertaking. The population of Hirta, the largest of the islands, never exceeded 200 people. Finding food on the island was often a challenge. The islanders would climb down the steep cliffs to harvest seabird eggs and babies. In 1930, food shortages and illness forced people to leave the island. The last 36 people living on Hirta were taken to Scotland's mainland. They were forced to get used to new things and new ways. They had never before seen a tree, river, paved road, or car!

What is the main idea?

A. People in Scotland are not used to trees or rivers.

B. When people from Hirta went to the mainland, their lives changed.

C. People in Hirta had to climb down steep cliffs to get to the beach.

Name _____ **Date** _____

Debbie's Diner

Ellen takes all her grandchildren out to eat once a month. Ellen has ten grandchildren. Ellen and her grandchildren always meet on the third Sunday of the month. The group has tried several restaurants. It's hard to find a restaurant that easily seats and serves large groups. Last month, everyone loved the service at Debbie's Diner. The group decided to go there again this month.

What is the main idea?

 A. Every month, Ellen takes her grandchildren out to eat at a restaurant that is good for big groups.

 B. Ellen takes her grandchildren out to a different restaurant every month.

 C. Ellen takes her grandchildren to Debbie's Diner because it is nearby.

Too Short!

Charlie went to the barbershop. When the barber asked him what kind of haircut he wanted, Charlie said, "Surprise me with something nice." The barber then cut Charlie's hair the same way he cuts other boys' hair. The barber spun the chair around so Charlie could see his new haircut. Charlie had a disappointed look on his face. "It's way too short!" cried Charlie. "Next time, I had better be more specific with how I want you to cut my hair."

What is the main idea?

 A. Charlie was disappointed because he told the barber exactly what he wanted, and the barber did not do it right.

 B. Charlie wanted his hair to look the same as the other boys'.

 C. Charlie didn't know what haircut he wanted and was unhappy afterwards.

Street Ball

In the evenings, all the neighborhood children play soccer. Because their local park is closed, the children play in the street. They have to watch out for cars. When someone yells, "Car!" everyone runs to the sidewalk. The children are looking forward to the park being open again. It is a much safer and bigger place to play.

What is the main idea?

A. The children enjoy playing soccer in the street because they like to yell, "Car!"

B. The children play soccer in the street because it's more fun than playing at the park.

C. The children can't wait for the park to open again so that they can safely play soccer.

Jumping Over Obstacles

Charlotte Brown is a pole-vaulter. Using her long pole, she has jumped over a bar 11 feet, 6 inches high! Brown is also legally blind. She says her vision is like looking down two black straws. Brown reads and writes in Braille. Brown can see the difference between light and dark, so her coach lays down artificial turf next to her lane. The turf is a light color compared to the dark running lane. The color contrast helps Brown stay in her lane. She also counts her steps before she jumps.

What is the main idea?

A. Pole-vaulters use a long pole to jump over a bar.

B. Charlotte Brown's poor vision hasn't stopped her from pole-vaulting.

C. Charlotte Brown has a coach who helps her.

Name _____ **Date** _____

Camera Man

Dave's favorite thing to do is take pictures. He has three special cameras that he uses for different purposes. One camera is so small that it fits in his pocket. He always has it with him. Dave also has an underwater camera. He likes to take pictures of his family when they swim. His third camera takes the best pictures. He uses it for taking the pictures that he enters into contests. One day, Dave hopes that he will win first place.

What is the main idea?

 A. Taking all kinds of pictures is Dave's hobby.
 B. Dave has unusual cameras.
 C. Dave takes his small camera everywhere with him.

Water Pups

A baby shark is called a pup. When pups are born, they are immediately ready to take care of themselves. Sometimes, if they don't swim away fast enough, the mother shark will eat them! Most shark species give birth to live pups, but about 40% of the shark population lays eggs. The eggs are laid in a protective case. The protective cases are often called "mermaid's purses." Some egg cases have tendrils, or strings, attached. The tendrils can be used to attach the case to seaweed, coral, or the ocean floor.

What is the main idea?

 A. Most shark species lay eggs in mermaid's purses.
 B. Sharks may have live pups or lay eggs.
 C. Mother sharks are not good mothers.

Name _____ **Date** _____

Super Swimmers

Water polo is a team sport that has similar rules as soccer and hockey. It is played in a swimming pool by two teams that try to throw a ball into a goal in order to score points. Since the sport is played in deep water, all players must constantly swim and tread water. Each team consists of six field players and one goalkeeper. The goalies are the only players who are allowed to touch the ball with both hands. The team that scores the most goals wins the game.

What is the main idea?

A. Water polo is a team water sport that has similar rules to both soccer and hockey.

B. Only the goalies in a water polo game can touch the ball with both hands.

C. Because water polo is played in deep water, all players must constantly swim and tread water.

Bike Dreams

Beside a tree, Andrew sat alone, watching the other children ride their bikes. One child was riding his red bike on the sidewalk. Another child could do wheelies and spin around. All the children in the neighborhood could do donuts. Isabell was riding her silver bike. She could jump the ramp and land a bunny hop. Andrew really wanted his own bicycle.

What is the main idea?

A. Andrew couldn't ride his bike because he was eating donuts by a tree.

B. Watching the neighborhood children ride their bikes made Andrew want his own bike.

C. Andrew wanted his own bike so he could learn what a bunny hop is.

Name _____ **Date** _____

Up and Away

Roger had always wanted to ride in a hot-air balloon. He saved enough money for his ticket by doing various jobs for the neighbors. It took a long time, but Roger finally had enough money. Roger wasn't nervous when he got into the basket. The higher the balloon climbed, the more Roger enjoyed the ride. Roger liked the feeling of peace and serenity as he soared over the hills. The view at sunrise was beautiful from up high.

What is the main idea?

A. Roger couldn't believe how quiet the ride was in the hot-air balloon.

B. Roger wasn't nervous when he rode in a hot-air balloon.

C. Roger earned enough money to take a very enjoyable ride.

Portrait Problems

The family went to a portrait studio. The family wanted a picture of everyone smiling. Things weren't working out because the baby kept crying, the children kept texting their friends, and the parents kept trying to make the children smile. Then the photographer asked, "How many bricks does it take to complete a brick building?" The children and the parents thought for a moment. They all smiled when they heard the answer, and that was when the photographer quickly snapped the picture. The answer was, "Only one—the last one."

What is the main idea?

A. The photographer was finally able to make everyone smile for the photograph.

B. The family picture didn't work out because the children kept texting their friends.

C. To understand the riddle, one had to pay attention to the word "complete."

Name _____ Date _____

Turtle Tales

Did you know that temperature determines whether a baby turtle becomes a male or female? First, a mother turtle chooses a sandy, sunny spot near a pond. She then digs an L-shaped hole and fills it with eggs. Males hatch from the eggs in the warmest part of the nest. The eggs in the cooler area will likely be females. Some years, if the summer has a very long hot or cold spell, the turtles will all be the same gender.

What is the main idea?

  A. Temperature in a turtle nest determines the gender of the baby turtles.
  B. The mother turtle digs an L-shaped hole in which she lays her eggs.
  C. Sometimes, all the baby turtles in a nest are the same gender.

Different Answers

Laurel and Chad's teacher would always say, "Each question has only one correct answer." Laurel and Chad thought of a way to show their teacher this wasn't so. All day long, Laurel and Chad asked their teacher the same question. They asked it many times. Each time their teacher gave a different answer, but each time the answer was correct! Laurel and Chad said, "We asked you the same question all day long, and each time you gave us a different answer. All your different answers were correct because you told us what time it was!"

What is the main idea?

  A. Laurel and Chad didn't know how to tell time, so they asked their teacher what time it was.
  B. Laurel and Chad wanted their teacher to answer different questions all day long.
  C. All day long, Laurel and Chad asked their teacher what time it was to show that sometimes one question can have more than one correct answer.

Name _____ **Date** _____

Bad Day at the Beach

Brandon loves going to the beach. Building sandcastles is his favorite thing to do. The only thing he doesn't like about going to the beach is having to put on sunblock. He says that he doesn't like the way it feels. One day, Brandon was playing at the beach for hours without wearing any sunblock. He realized later that wearing sunblock felt a lot better on his skin than the awful sunburn he got from not wearing it. Now he wears sunblock every time he goes to the beach.

What is the main idea?

A. Brandon doesn't like the way sunblock feels on his skin.

B. After getting a bad sunburn, Brandon learned the importance of wearing sunblock.

C. Brandon's favorite thing to do at the beach is building sandcastles.

Hang Up

Using a cell phone while riding a bike or driving a car is not safe. Using cell phones to talk, text, and/or go online is easy because cell phones can be used almost anywhere. Although it may seem easy to use a cell phone while trying to ride a bike or drive, it should not be done. Bike riders and drivers need to be focused on the road ahead of them. Texting and driving causes distracted drivers, and a distracted driver is unsafe. The texting driver is more likely to cause an accident.

What is the main idea?

A. Using a cell phone to talk, text, and go online is always easy.

B. Using a cell phone while driving or riding a bike is not safe.

C. Bike riders and drivers need to focus on what their friends are telling them so they know where to go.

Name _____ **Date** _____

Cool Shades

Wearing sunglasses outdoors is a good idea. Not only do sunglasses look stylish, but they can help to protect your eyes as well. The sun is very strong and bright. Constant exposure to sunlight can lead to various eye conditions. The sun gives off UV rays that can harm your eyes. Sunglasses can block these powerful rays. Wearing sunglasses will protect your eyes and make it easier to see on a bright day.

What is the main idea?

A. The sun gives off very harmful rays.

B. Sunglasses are a stylish way to enjoy the outdoors.

C. Sunglasses protect your eyes from the sun.

Presidential Prerequisites

Not everyone can run for president of the United States. People who are interested must meet three requirements. First, the potential candidate must be at least 35 years old. Second, that person must have been born in the United States. Third, the person must have lived in the U.S. for at least 14 years. Only after these requirements have been met may a person run for office.

What is the main idea?

A. One must be elected if they want to be president of the United States.

B. Any U.S. citizen may run for president if he or she so desires.

C. Before running for president, one must meet three requirements.

Name _____   **Date** _____

Meg the Mower

Meg was looking forward to turning 13. That's when her parents said she could babysit. Meg thought babysitting would be a good summer job. Soon after turning 13, Meg's aunt hired her to babysit her son Jake. Jake's long tantrum and food-throwing habit caused Meg to change her mind. "Maybe mowing lawns would be a better job for me," she thought.

What is the main idea?

A. Meg thought babysitting would be a good job for her—until she had a bad babysitting experience.

B. Meg thought that mowing lawns would be a better job because it pays more.

C. Meg wanted a summer job so she could buy her own lawn mower.

Blue-Blooded

Octopuses and squid both have blue blood. Why is their blood blue while ours is red? We have something called hemoglobin in our blood. Hemoglobin contains four iron atoms that bind to oxygen. This is how oxygen is carried around our blood stream. The iron is what makes our blood red. Octopuses and squid transport their oxygen with a different metal. Octopuses and squid don't use iron, they use copper. The copper makes their blood look blue.

What is the main idea?

A. Octopuses and squid both have blue blood.

B. The metal that carries oxygen in blood affects the color of the blood.

C. Different mammals have different colors of blood.

Name _____ **Date** _____

The Escape of Fu Manchu

Zookeepers were mad because, once again, Fu Manchu had gotten out of his cage. Fu Manchu was an orangutan. He was born and lived in the Omaha Zoo. At first, zookeepers thought someone was leaving a door unlocked. People were told that someone was going to lose his or her job for being so careless. Then someone saw Fu Manchu climb into an air vent and into a dry moat below. Then the clever orangutan yanked on the cage door until there was a little gap. After that, he slipped a piece of wire through the gap to unhook the latch that kept the door locked!

What is the main idea?

A. Orangutans are very clever apes.

B. Fu Manchu was able to escape from his cage several times before zookeepers found out how he did it.

C. An orangutan in Omaha was able to get a piece of wire from a careless zookeeper.

Tasty Trees

Sap from maple trees is used to make the tasty maple syrup that we use on our waffles and pancakes. To get sap from a maple tree, you must first drill a few holes into the tree trunk. Next, you put spouts into the holes. The sap runs out through the spouts and into buckets. After the sap has been collected, it is taken to a sugar house. This is where the sap is boiled for many hours until it eventually turns into maple syrup. It takes about forty gallons of sap to make one gallon of syrup.

What is the main idea?

A. To get sap from a maple tree, you must drill a few holes into the tree trunk.

B. Sap is boiled for many hours until it turns into maple syrup.

C. Sap from maple trees is used to make maple syrup.

Name _____   **Date** _____

Tryout Jitters

Joe wanted to play on the high school baseball team. He practiced every day to improve his pitching, hitting, and catching skills. When tryout day came, Joe was excited and nervous. When he arrived at school, he realized that he had forgotten his glove. Luckily, he was able to borrow a glove and still show that he was a good player. Joe was selected to be the team's first baseman.

What is the main idea?

   A. Joe wanted to be a pitcher on the baseball team.
   B. Joe couldn't try out for the baseball team because he forgot his glove.
   C. Joe practiced baseball each day and earned a spot on the team.

Going Green

Kate saves plastic bottles for recycling. She takes the bottles to a place where they give her a nickel for each small bottle she brings in. She gets a dime for every large bottle she brings in. Kate uses the recycling money to buy new beverages.

What is the main idea?

   A. Kate only recycles large plastic bottles because she gets a dime for each bottle.
   B. Kate recycles plastic bottles at a place that gives her money for them.
   C. Kate recycles plastic bottles so that they don't end up in landfills.

Name _____ Date _____

Hatching Memories

A young girl named Nicky visited the zoo last month. While she was there, several penguin eggs hatched. Nicky was one of the first people to see the baby penguins. She happened to be near the penguin exhibit when the baby chicks broke out of their shells. She was surprised to see that the chicks didn't have feathers. Nicky was happy to be part of this very exciting event.

What is the main idea?

A. Nicky was one of the first people to see the new baby penguins at the zoo.

B. Nicky was working at the zoo when the baby penguins hatched.

C. Nicky was volunteering in the penguin exhibit and got to watch the baby penguins hatch.

No Vote from Mom?

At school, Matt read about John Adams and Abraham Lincoln. When Matt was done reading, he thought, "It seems that these two men were great presidents." Then Matt read that Adams' mother didn't vote for him when he ran for president. Lincoln's mother didn't vote for Lincoln when he ran, either. Matt thought, "Were these presidents really so great if even their own mothers wouldn't vote for them?" Then Matt remembered—their mothers couldn't vote for them! Women weren't allowed to vote until 1920.

What is the main idea?

A. Before 1920, women could not vote.

B. If a president is really great, his mother will vote for him.

C. John Adams and Abraham Lincoln were both great presidents.

Name _____ Date _____

After-School Activities

Dwayne goes to after-school care every day for a few hours. On school days, both of his parents work until 5:00 p.m. Dwayne does his homework immediately after school. Then he plays games with his friends.

When does Dwayne play games?

A. before he does his homework
B. after he does his homework
C. at 5:00 p.m.

Balancing Meals

Eating balanced meals every day is important. A balanced meal has foods from each food group. Fruits, such as apples and oranges, should be eaten daily, as should vegetables, like broccoli and spinach. Fruits and vegetables have valuable vitamins that our bodies need in order to stay healthy. We should also eat plenty of whole grains, like bread, for extra energy. Proteins, such as meat and beans, are important in building strong muscles. Dairy products are also important to help build healthy bones.

What will eating whole grains give you?

A. extra energy
B. strong muscles
C. healthy bones

Name _____ **Date** _____

Support Our School

As a fundraiser, the fourth-grade class was selling smoothies for two dollars each. They were raising money for a field trip. Andrea asked her dad if she could buy a smoothie. He gave her six dollars and told her to get one of each flavor for them to share.

How much did each smoothie cost?

A. two dollars
B. three dollars
C. six dollars

Healthy Habits

Cameron and Jane made salads for lunch. They started by filling a bowl with lettuce. They added bean sprouts and shredded carrots. They next poured some ranch dressing on top. Cameron and Jane finished making their salads by sprinkling a little pepper on them.

When did Cameron and Jane sprinkle pepper?

A. before adding the bean sprouts
B. before pouring the ranch dressing
C. after pouring the ranch dressing

Name _____   **Date** _____

Standing Room Only

Every seat in the room was taken. Many people were standing up. Some people were even sitting on the floor. The lights dimmed at exactly six o'clock. The talent show was about to begin. Everyone cheered when the students took the stage.

When did the show start?

A. at seven o'clock

B. at six o'clock

C. at five o'clock

Surviving the Cold

Some species of bats hibernate. When they hibernate, many bats can allow their bodies to cool close to the freezing point. There is one kind of bat that can withstand temperatures that are below the freezing point. Out of all species of bats, this bat has the thickest fur, and it can survive even if some of its tissues freeze! When the temperature is low, this bat has the slowest heartbeat. The bat is called the North American red bat. The North American red bat has a higher red blood cell count than any other species of bat.

What is special about the North American red bat?

A. Out of all the bat species, it has the thickest fur.

B. Out of all the bat species, it has the highest heartbeat.

C. Out of all the bat species, it is the only one to hibernate.

Name _____ **Date** _____

Summer Vacation

The Ramirez family went to Lake Toofun for summer vacation. They go there every year. They towed their boat behind their truck. As soon as they arrived, they unloaded their things. Then they took their boat out on the lake to go swimming and waterskiing.

What did the Ramirez family do as soon as they arrived?

A. took their boat out on the lake

B. went waterskiing

C. unloaded their things

Secret Savings

Layla saves her dollar bills and coins in a piggy bank. The piggy bank looks like a book. It looks like a book so that it can be hidden in plain sight on a bookshelf. Layla is saving her money to buy a new video game. The video game she wants costs $25 plus tax. When Layla's piggy bank has close to $30, she will ask her mom to take her to the store.

What is Layla saving for?

A. a new piggy bank

B. a new book

C. a new video game

Name _____ **Date** _____

Dancing Raisins

The teacher was doing a science experiment. She poured lemon-lime soda into a glass, and then she dropped in a few raisins. The bubbles from the soda stuck to the raisins, making them float. Once the bubbles popped, the raisins sank. The raisins went up and down in the glass several times.

When did the teacher drop in the raisins?

A. after she poured in the soda

B. before she poured in the soda

C. after all the bubbles in the soda were gone

Grandma's Gift

Today is Ricky's birthday. He received several gifts and a card from his grandma. In the card, Ricky found several coupons. One coupon said, "This is good for a free trip with Grandma to the movies!" Another coupon said, "This is good for one free popcorn and candy at the movie theater."

What was in Ricky's card?

A. coupons

B. movie tickets

C. candy

Name _____ **Date** _____

Talented Twins

Harold and Hazel are twins. They have been taking piano lessons since they were seven years old. When they started, they didn't know what the difference was between all the piano keys. Harold would bang on the white keys while Hazel would pound on the black keys. The sound they produced was nothing but a horrible racket. Now the twins are twelve. They know how to read music, and each can play the piano very well.

When did Hazel start taking piano lessons?

A. at age seven
B. at age eleven
C. at age twelve

Long-Distance Flyer

What bird sees more daylight than any other bird? No other bird sees as much daylight in a year as the Arctic tern. The tern spends the summer in the Arctic at a time when the sun doesn't set. After breeding, it flies south to the other side of the world and experiences a second summer. The bird doesn't fly in a straight path. That way, it can take advantage of the way winds blow. Arctic terns can live to be 30 years old. This means that, in their lifetime, they can fly about 1.5 million miles. This distance is the same as about three round trips to the moon!

When does the Arctic tern fly south?

A. after flying 1.5 million miles
B. after returning from the moon
C. after breeding in the Arctic

Name _____ **Date** _____

Mountain Bike

Aiden was given a mountain bike for his eleventh birthday. He had asked for a mountain bike so that he could go riding with his father. Aiden loves his new bike. It is red, yellow, and black, and it has big tires. Tomorrow, Aiden and his dad are excited to go on a seven-mile ride.

When did Aiden get a mountain bike?

A. for Christmas
B. for his birthday
C. when he got all good grades

Brain Freeze

Yesterday, Lily and Jayden went to an ice-cream shop. Lily ordered two scoops of chocolate ice cream served in a waffle bowl. Jayden ordered one scoop of vanilla served in a sugar cone. Lily ate her ice cream quickly. Jayden must have eaten his ice cream too quickly—he grabbed his head and made a funny face. "Brain freeze!" he yelled.

What did Jayden order?

A. one scoop of chocolate
B. one scoop of vanilla
C. two scoops of vanilla

Name _____ **Date** _____

Grape Idea!

Emma was going to a costume party held at her friend Jose's house. Emma first tried on a bunny costume that she already had, but it was too small. That's when she decided to make a new costume. Emma blew up a lot of small, purple balloons. Then, she changed into a purple sweatshirt and purple sweatpants. After she was dressed, Emma attached the balloons to her clothes. She went to the party as a bunch of grapes!

Where was Emma going?

A. to a birthday party
B. to buy grapes
C. to her friend's house

Mystery Baby

Wendy woke up to the sound of a crying baby. Wendy thought it was strange because she doesn't have a baby brother or sister. Then Wendy found out it was her older brother's alarm. He changed his alarm to a "cry" setting because he knew it would get him right out of bed!

What woke Wendy up?

A. the sound of her brother yelling
B. the sound of a baby laughing
C. the sound of a baby crying

Name _____ **Date** _____

Best Field Trip Ever!

The fourth-grade class went on a field trip to Wonderville Amusement Park. The students were put in groups of four, and each group had a parent helper who was required to stay with it. The students went on several fast rides, and they even got to eat cotton candy.

Where did the class go?

A. Wonderworld Amusement Park
B. Wonderville Amusement Park
C. Wonderland Amusement Park

Tremendous Tower

The Eiffel Tower is a famous structure in Paris, France. It was built as the entrance arch for the 1889 World's Fair. The tower was the tallest man-made structure in the world for 41 years. It is constructed from iron, and it is 1,050 feet high. When it is really hot, the tower is six inches higher! That's because the iron expands in the heat!

Why and when was the Eiffel Tower built?

A. as the entry tower for the 1889 France Fair
B. as the entrance arch for the 1898 World's Fair
C. as the entrance arch for the 1889 World's Fair

Name _____ **Date** _____

Unexpected Workout

George and his family live in Washington, D.C. They live in a tall building. The power went out in their building last week, so the elevators weren't working. The family had to climb up several flights of stairs to get to their apartment.

When did the power go out?

  A. last week

  B. yesterday

  C. two days ago

Giving Thanks

Frank's mother, Joan, is a doctor. Joan doesn't want to work on Thanksgiving Day, but it is her turn. Each year, Joan and the doctors she works with take turns working on all the major holidays. This is the year Joan is supposed to work on Thanksgiving. Frank said to his mother, "Let's celebrate Thanksgiving on Friday instead of Thursday. We can still give thanks for all the food, and we can still be thankful we are all healthy."

When will Joan have to work?

  A. on Friday

  B. on Thursday

  C. on Mother's Day

Name _____ **Date** _____

Wolves of the Sea

Orcas, also called killer whales, belong to the dolphin family. They have a black back, a white chest, and a white patch near each eye. Orcas are at the top of their food chain because they do not have any natural predators. They live in small groups called *pods*, and they can be found in all oceans. Orcas are sometimes called the wolves of the sea because, like wolves, they hunt in packs. At times, orcas will even hunt sharks.

What family do orcas belong to?

A. the whale family
B. the shark family
C. the dolphin family

Movie Mistakes

Ben and Erica rented a movie. The movie had dinosaurs in it. Ben and Erica put a bag of popcorn in the microwave when they got home. They ate popcorn and watched the movie. Ben and Erica liked the movie, but they thought the filmmakers needed to do more research on dinosaurs. Some of the flying dinosaurs in the movie were larger than a school bus. Ben and Erica knew that the largest flying dinosaur was only about four feet long.

When did Ben and Erica microwave popcorn?

A. when the movie was over
B. when they got home
C. before they rented a movie

Name _____ **Date** _____

Small Friends

Hamsters are small animals. Many people keep them as pets. Hamsters are nocturnal animals. This means that they sleep during the day and are awake at night. During the night, many pet hamsters can be found running on exercise wheels. Hamsters have very poor eyesight. They rely on scent in order to find their way. Hamsters have scent glands on their bodies. Hamsters will leave a scent trail by rubbing on rocks and other objects in their path.

When are hamsters awake?

A. at night

B. during the day

C. in the morning

Mighty Maine

Fifty states comprise the United States, and each state is unique. Maine is a New England state. It joined the Union on March 15, 1820, as the 23rd state. Maine is famous for its lobsters. More lobsters are harvested in Maine than any other state. Maine is the only state with a one-syllable name, and it is also the only state with just one other state on its border. The only state Maine borders is New Hampshire. Maine has 3,166 islands.

What makes Maine unique?

A. It is the only state with a one-syllable name.

B. It is the only state with just two other states on its border.

C. It is ranked 23rd in lobster harvesting and sales.

Name _____ **Date** _____

Safe Swimming

Swimming pools are fun for people to play in, but they can also be very dangerous. It is good for swimming pools to have fences around them. If someone falls into a pool and doesn't know how to swim, he or she can drown. Swimming is great exercise. If you swim hard, you will burn off more calories than if you walk or bike.

It is good for swimming pools to have _____ around them.

   A. bike paths

   B. fences

   C. grass

Which One Are You?

Molly and Holly are twins. Molly was born six minutes before Holly. They look almost exactly alike. The girls are in the same class. They like to come to school dressed alike. Their teacher sometimes has trouble telling them apart.

When was Holly born?

   A. six minutes after Molly

   B. at exactly the same time as Molly

   C. six minutes before Molly

Muy Delicioso

Kyle and Marissa like Mexican food. They like going to a Mexican restaurant near their house. They go with their big brother. At the restaurant, chips and salsa are put on every table. Marissa thinks the salsa is too spicy. Marissa and Kyle's big brother thinks it is too salty. Kyle thinks the salsa is delicious.

Who thinks the salsa is spicy?

A. Marissa

B. Kyle and Marissa's big brother

C. Kyle

Forever Stamp

Postage stamps are required when mailing letters. Postage stamps have become more expensive over time. For this reason, the "Forever Stamp" was created. People buy Forever Stamps for the same price as regular stamps, but if the price of stamps ever goes up, the Forever Stamp can still be used.

How much do Forever Stamps cost?

A. the same as regular stamps

B. more than regular stamps

C. less than regular stamps

Name _____ **Date** _____

Dance Partners

Jada signed up for a dance class that meets every Thursday afternoon. On the first day, Jada made a new friend. Jada and her new friend, Olivia, became dance partners. They performed the opening dance at their dance recital.

When does Jada have dance class?

A. every Tuesday afternoon

B. every Thursday night

C. every Thursday afternoon

Caring Crabs

There is only one crab that takes care of its young. It lives in the mountain forests of Jamaica. This tiny land crab is less than an inch wide. It is called the bromeliad crab because it lives in pools of water that form in the leaves of bromeliad plants. The female crab lays about 90 eggs in the water. She keeps the water clean by taking out dead leaves. She also adds calcium to the water by adding snail shells. When the eggs hatch, she feeds her young cockroaches and millipedes.

What does the mother crab add to the water?

A. dead leaves

B. snail shells

C. bromeliad plants

Name _____ **Date** _____

Super Scholar

The teacher asked the class a social studies question. Jasmin raised her hand quickly so that she could be the first to _____.

Which word best completes the sentence?

A. exit

B. ask

C. respond

Pobody Is Nerfect

My sister said she lost her favorite shirt and asked if I knew where it was. I asked my sister to _____ what it looked like. She said that her shirt was blue, and that the words "Pobody Is Nerfect" was printed in black letters on the front.

Which word best completes the sentence?

A. describe

B. understand

C. find

Name _____ **Date** _____

Brotherly Love?

Will <u>taunted</u> his baby sister by holding her milk bottle in front of her and then pulling it away. This made her cry. When Will's mother saw what Will was doing, she was disappointed. She asked, "How would you feel if someone did that to you with something you wanted?"

The underlined word means

A. fed.
B. changed.
C. teased.

Tastes Like Sofa

When Vanessa got home, she noticed that her dog had chewed up her brand new sofa. She was <u>furious</u>! The look on her face showed exactly how unhappy she was.

Which word can best replace the underlined word?

A. thrilled
B. angry
C. excited

Name _____ **Date** _____

Making the Family Fit

Hailey was framing her family portrait. When she placed the picture into the frame, it was a bit too big to fit. She had to <u>decrease</u> the size of the picture by using scissors to trim one edge.

The underlined word means

  A. make bigger.

  B. make smaller.

  C. glue down.

Nice Day for a Stroll

Sam saw his sister <u>sauntering</u> down the path. She looked so carefree that he wasn't sure he wanted to tell her that she had just stepped over a snake!

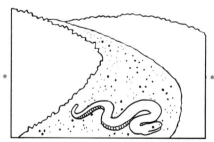

The underlined word means

  A. walking in a slow and relaxed manner.

  B. walking cautiously and with fear.

  C. walking quickly and noisily.

Name _____ **Date** _____

Sweet Science

Sophia made a _____ of sugar and water. She stirred it quickly to see if the grains of sugar would dissolve in the water.

Which word best completes the sentence?

A. mixture

B. mountain

C. dinner

Pick a Prize

Franklin was asked to pick a _____ prize out of the treasure box today. He will have to close his eyes and then reach in to select one. Franklin is hoping he'll pick the blue pair of sunglasses as his prize, but he also thinks the black eye patch is cool. I wonder which prize he will get.

Which word best completes the sentence?

A. blue

B. random

C. expensive

Name _____ **Date** _____

Ready for Winter

Mason thought that his friend Robert was dressed in a <u>bizarre</u> way. Robert was wearing pants, a thick jacket, and a snow hat in the middle of summer.

Which word can best replace the underlined word?

  A. nice
  B. wonderful
  C. strange

A Wacky Habit

Carly has an unusual habit. At dinner, she likes to eat each food item on a _____ plate. For example, she puts salad on one plate, chicken on another plate, and corn on another. She doesn't like them together on the same plate.

Which word best completes the sentence?

  A. paper
  B. round
  C. separate

Reaching the Summit

Samantha and Liam went for a long hike up Mount Steepside. The two friends were proud of themselves when they reached the <u>summit</u> after four hours. They enjoyed the view and some cold water before hiking back down the mountain.

Which word can best replace the underlined word?

A. bottom

B. top

C. trail

Grandma's Stories

My grandmother became very <u>feeble</u> as she grew older. She was no longer able to ride her bicycle or run on the beach, but she could still tell wonderful stories.

Which word can best replace the underlined word?

A. weak

B. fast

C. active

Name _____ **Date** _____

Sweet Treats

Mark and Elizabeth were making cookies. They lined up the following ingredients on the kitchen counter: flour, sugar, eggs, salt, baking soda, and vanilla. The recipe said to _____ the wet and the dry ingredients.

Which word best completes the sentence?

A. combine

B. chew

C. touch

Magical Party

A magician was at Jennifer's tenth birthday party. The magician was doing magic tricks for Jennifer and her guests. The magician asked for three people to _____ in his next trick. They had to pull ribbons out of his hat.

Which word best completes the sentence?

A. argue

B. disappear

C. participate

Name _____ **Date** _____

Stars and Stripes

The 50 stars on the United States flag _____ the 50 states. There is a star on the flag for every state in the country. There are 13 stripes on the flag, too. Each of the 13 stripes stands for one of the original 13 colonies.

Which word best completes the sentence?

   A. control

   B. represent

   C. visit

Discovered Talent

Gabe made a new _____ this morning. While he was making funny faces at himself in the mirror, he found out that he could touch his nose with the tip of his tongue! He never knew he could do such an interesting trick.

Which word best completes the sentence?

   A. idea

   B. recipe

   C. discovery

Name _____   **Date** _____

Good Science

While getting ready for this year's science fair, Kim had a _____ of last year's science fair. She remembered the winner. Last year's winner did an experiment with rubber bands. He tested how much weight they could hold before breaking.

Which word best completes the sentence?
- **A.** sample
- **B.** flashback
- **C.** plan

Mom's New Recipe

Braden thought the _____ coming from the kitchen smelled wonderful. The smell was making his mouth water! Then Braden found out what was making the smell. It was an octopus-and-snail stew!

Which word best completes the sentence?
- **A.** aroma
- **B.** food
- **C.** meal

Name _____ **Date** _____

Foliage Fashion

Maria was walking down the street. She was going to her favorite bookstore. As she walked, Maria saw her _____ in a store window. That's when she noticed that she had a leaf stuck in her hair. Maria brushed the leaf out before going into the bookstore.

Which word best completes the sentence?

  A. computer
  B. mother
  C. reflection

A Little Research

Before Daniel bought a ticket to see the new movie, he first watched a _____ of it. Daniel wanted to make sure that he would be interested in watching it. Daniel didn't want to waste his money. Before he paid to go in, he wanted to be certain he would like the movie.

Which word best completes the sentence?

  A. preview
  B. purchase
  C. theater

Name _____ **Date** _____

Finding the Area

Robin learned the _____ for finding the area of a rectangle. It is length multiplied by width. Then Robin started her homework. Robin solved the first problem easily. She said, "The rectangle is three inches long. It is five inches wide. Three times five is fifteen. The area of the rectangle is fifteen square inches."

Which word best completes the sentence?
  A. number
  B. formula
  C. division

Missing Recess

The class made too much noise yesterday. As a _____, the teacher made the class stay in the classroom when the recess bell rang. The students had to work quietly for five minutes before they were allowed to go outside.

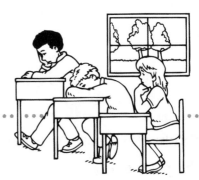

Which word best completes the sentence?
  A. consequence
  B. reward
  C. trouble

Name _____   **Date** _____

Spelling Pride

Arturo was proud of himself. He had just won an award for being the best speller at his school. Arturo wanted to frame his award and _____ it in his room. He considered hanging it above his desk right next to the picture of his dog, Pepper.

SUPER SPELLER
AWARD
Arturo
☆ ☆ ☆ ☆

Which word best completes the sentence?

A. display

B. break

C. hide

Flying High

Colton was amazed by what he was reading. Colton read that the Rüppell's vulture was thought to be the highest-flying bird. How high could it fly? It was once seen _____ 36,100 feet above sea level! "That's higher than the tallest mountain in the world," Colton thought.

Which word best completes the sentence?

A. shocking

B. landing

C. soaring

Name _____ **Date** _____

Every Drop Counts

Trevor was thinking about ways he could _____ water. He decided to take shorter showers. He also wouldn't leave the water running when he was brushing his teeth.

Which word best completes the sentence?
  A. complete
  B. create
  C. conserve

Watch Closely!

Rosa and Noah carefully _____ the way the artist drew the picture of the man's face. They watched every move. They didn't want to miss a step. They wanted to memorize how to draw it so that they could practice later.

Which word best completes the sentence?
  A. cleaned
  B. observed
  C. brushed

Name _____ **Date** _____

Daily Warm-Up

As the students walked into their classroom, they saw a math problem on the board. The teacher asked the students to immediately begin working on it. The students quietly sat down and picked up their pencils. Then they began to figure out the _____. It was 4,678.

Which word best completes the sentence?
- **A.** solved
- **B.** solution
- **C.** calendar

Book Club

Henry and Mia read the same book. It was about a family of fishermen. Even though there were some sad parts in the story, it got much happier by the _____.

Which word best completes the sentence?
- **A.** beginning
- **B.** character
- **C.** conclusion

Name _____ **Date** _____

Little Stars

Mrs. Denver's class was putting on a performance in the theater for the rest of the school. Many of the students' parents were in the _____. Everyone had come to watch their children. They all wanted to see the short skits that the children had written by themselves.

Room 25 Presents: I've Got Talent!

AUDITORIUM

Which word best completes the sentence?

A. audience
B. show
C. classroom

Mind Your Manners

Addie and Max were always _____. They always said "please" and "thank you." They remembered their manners when eating, too. They always put their napkins on their laps, and they wouldn't start eating until their hostess had taken the first bite.

Which word best completes the sentence?

A. comfortable
B. courteous
C. crazy

Name _____ Date _____

City Living

Which <u>two</u> statements are **facts**?

A. Speed limits are slower near schools.
B. Traffic tickets can involve paying fines.
C. It is better to drive than to ride your bike.

Beach Days

Which <u>two</u> statements are **opinions**?

A. Playing in the sand at the beach is too messy.
B. Some people build sandcastles at the beach.
C. Swimming pools are more fun than the beach.

Chocolate Milk

Which <u>two</u> statements are **facts**?

A. Chocolate milk is only served in some schools.
B. Chocolate milk is more delicious than white milk.
C. White milk has fewer ingredients than chocolate milk.

Water Sports

Which <u>two</u> statements are **opinions**?

A. There are multiple swimming events in the Olympic Games.
B. Swimming is the best Olympic sport to watch.
C. The backstroke events are the hardest races for swimmers.

Air Jordan

Which <u>two</u> statements are **facts**?

A. Michael Jordan is a six-time NBA champion.
B. Michael Jordan is the greatest basketball player of all time.
C. Michael Jordan is a retired basketball player.

Name That Dog

Which <u>two</u> statements are **opinions**?

A. Bella, Molly, and Lucy should not have been the top three names for female dogs in 2013.
B. It is hard to believe that the top three male dog names for 2013 were Max, Buddy, and Rocky.
C. VPI Pet Insurance kept a list of the top dog names for 2013.

Name _____ Date _____

Now I Know My ABCs

Which <u>two</u> statements are **facts**?

A. There are 26 letters in the English alphabet.

B. The letters *A, E, I, O,* and *U* are vowels.

C. Most children like to sing the alphabet song.

Red, White, and Blue

Which <u>two</u> statements are **opinions**?

A. Fireworks are the best part of a Fourth of July celebration.

B. Independence Day is celebrated on July 4th.

C. People should get presents on July 4th.

Some Pig!

Which <u>two</u> statements are **facts**?

A. All students enjoy reading *Charlotte's Web* in school.

B. *Charlotte's Web* was written by E. B. White.

C. *Charlotte's Web* is an award-winning children's novel.

Bright Ideas

Which <u>two</u> statements are **opinions**?

A. The light bulb is the greatest invention of all time.

B. Thomas Edison invented the light bulb.

C. Inventors are the most important people in science.

A Day to Celebrate

Which <u>two</u> statements are **facts**?

A. Some people eat cake at birthday parties.

B. People have birthdays once a year.

C. People should have cake at birthday parties.

February

Which <u>two</u> statements are **opinions**?

A. It rains too much during the month of February.

B. February is the shortest month of the year.

C. February is a great month to have a birthday.

Name _____ **Date** _____

Creepy, Crawly, and Amazing

Which <u>two</u> statements are **facts**?

A. A spider's eight legs make it look unnatural.

B. Spider silk is the strongest of all natural-made fibers.

C. When you compare a spider's dragline and a strand of steel the same size, the spider's silk is stronger.

Roses Are Red . . . and White

Which <u>two</u> statements are **opinions**?

A. Red roses are the best gift for someone you love.

B. Roses come in different colors.

C. White roses smell too sweet.

Picture Pages

Which <u>two</u> statements are **facts**?

A. The person who draws pictures for a book is called the illustrator.

B. *The Cat in the Hat* has really good illustrations.

C. The writer of *The Cat in the Hat* was also the illustrator.

Morning Ride

Which <u>two</u> statements are **opinions**?

A. Riding a bike to school is more fun than walking to school.

B. Children should not ride bikes to school.

C. Riding a bike to school is usually faster than walking to school.

Out of This World

Which <u>two</u> statements are **facts**?

A. We should go to Jupiter because it is the largest planet.

B. You would weigh about two and a half times your normal weight if you were on Jupiter.

C. More than 1,300 Earths could fit inside Jupiter.

Sleepy Solutions

Which <u>two</u> statements are **opinions**?

A. A king-size bed is bigger than a queen-size bed.

B. A king-size bed is more comfortable than a queen-size bed.

C. A twin-size bed is the perfect size for a young child.

Name _____   Date _____

Worldly Words

Which <u>two</u> statements are **facts**?

A. Words written in English are read from left to right.

B. We read from right to left when we read words written in Arabic.

C. It would be easier if all writing was read from left to right.

Typing Trouble

Which <u>two</u> statements are **opinions**?

A. The keys on a keyboard are not in alphabetical order.

B. Typing on a keyboard is hard when the typist is not looking.

C. The keys on a keyboard should be in alphabetical order.

Soccer or Football?

Which <u>two</u> statements are **facts**?

A. All soccer players should be allowed to use their hands to touch the ball when the ball is in play.

B. In a soccer game, when the ball is in play, only the goalies are allowed to use their hands to touch the ball.

C. In many countries, the game of soccer is called *football*.

Month by Month

Which <u>two</u> statements are **opinions**?

A. February is the worst winter month.

B. The best months of the year are when the flowers bloom.

C. January was named after Janus, the Roman god of beginnings and endings.

Add It Up

Which <u>two</u> statements are **facts**?

A. To find the perimeter of a square, you add the lengths of all the sides.

B. Finding the perimeter of a square is easy.

C. Perimeter is the distance around a polygon.

Big Cats

Which <u>two</u> statements are **opinions**?

A. The four largest cats are the lion, tiger, jaguar, and leopard.

B. Tigers are the best-looking big cats because they have stripes.

C. Lions, tigers, jaguars, and leopards are better than other cats because they are the only cats that can roar.

Same or Opposite?

Which <u>two</u> statements are **facts**?

A. *Synonyms* are words that have the same meaning.
B. Words that have opposite meanings are called *antonyms*.
C. It's easy to think of words that have opposite meanings.

Bike Smart

Which <u>two</u> statements are **opinions**?

A. Children under age five are too young to learn how to ride a bike.
B. Bike helmets should have more pads inside of them.
C. Many states have laws that require bike riders to wear helmets.

Turkey Day

Which <u>two</u> statements are **facts**?

A. Thanksgiving is the most important holiday of the year.
B. Thanksgiving is always on the fourth Thursday in November.
C. Thanksgiving is a national holiday.

Presidential Palace

Which <u>two</u> statements are **opinions**?

A. People should tour the White House when visiting Washington, D.C.
B. The president of the United States lives in the White House.
C. The White House should not have a private indoor pool.

Not Real Glass

Which <u>two</u> statements are **facts**?

A. The glass frog lives in Central and South America.
B. Glass frogs make really cool pets.
C. The glass frog's skin is so transparent that you can see some of its bones, muscles, and organs.

Borrowing Books

Which <u>two</u> statements are **opinions**?

A. The library does not have many good books to choose from.
B. Libraries should be open 24 hours a day, seven days a week.
C. At the library, people can check out books.

Name _____ **Date** _____

Two-Alarm Morning

Mindy had an important day at school today. She had a reading test first thing in the morning. Mindy didn't want to be late, so <u>she set two different alarm clocks for 6:30 a.m.</u> She jumped out of bed when they both went off this morning!

The underlined statement is the **cause**. What is the **effect**?

A. Mindy woke up before the alarms went off.
B. Mindy jumped out of bed when the alarms went off.
C. Mindy had an important day at school today.

Lost and Found

Callahan was waiting in line for an amusement-park ride. <u>Near the line, he found a key lying on the ground.</u> Callahan picked up the key, wondering what to do. He heard several people nearby talking about looking for a missing key. "I found the key!" Callahan shouted. "Thank you very much," said a woman. "That's my car key."

The underlined statement is the **effect**. What is the **cause**?

A. A woman lost her key by the amusement-park ride.
B. A woman thanked the boy for finding her car key.
C. A woman told several people that a boy found her key.

Hot Walk

Last July, my parents' van broke down on the way home from our family vacation. <u>My dad walked one mile to the nearest gas station.</u> The rest of us waited in a nearby grocery store to stay out of the heat. Poor Dad—he was sweating when he returned.

The underlined statement is the **cause**. What is the **effect**?

A. The van broke down during the family vacation.
B. Dad was sad that the gas station was closed.
C. Dad was sweating from walking in the heat.

Name _____ **Date** _____

Family Wardrobe

Marty had outgrown a lot of his clothes. Some of his pants were too short, and some of his shirts were too tight. <u>Marty passed on to his cousin Alex some clothes that didn't fit</u>. Alex said if he outgrew the clothes and if they were still in good condition, he would pass them on to his own little brother.

The underlined statement is the **effect**. What is the **cause**?

A. Marty didn't like how those clothes looked.
B. Some clothes were too small for Marty to wear.
C. Marty wanted to give his clothes to his little brother.

Making Green

Brianna was painting a picture of her backyard. She ran out of green paint while painting the grass. <u>Brianna mixed a little blue and yellow paint together</u>. By mixing the blue and yellow paint, Brianna was able to make enough green paint to finish the grass and add the trees.

The underlined statement is the **cause**. What is the **effect**?

A. Brianna couldn't finish her painting.
B. Brianna was painting a picture of her back yard.
C. Brianna was able to finish the grass and add the trees.

Wild Eyes

When we look at something, both of our eyes look at the same thing. We cannot make one eye go one way while the other eye goes in the opposite direction. Chameleons are not like you and me. Chameleons are a kind of lizard. Their eyes move independently of each other. This means that <u>one eye can be looking for insects to eat while the other eye can be watching out for predators</u>!

The underlined statement is the **effect**. What is the **cause**?

A. Chameleon eyes move independently of each other.
B. Chameleons are a type of lizard.
C. Chameleons need to find insects to eat.

Name _____ Date _____

Young Scientists

Trent and Becky were doing a science experiment. They were testing different objects to see if the objects would sink or float. Trent and Becky decided to see if a crayon would float. They predicted that it would. Trent and Becky filled up the sink with water; then, they dropped a purple crayon into the water. The crayon immediately sank to the bottom of the sink.

The underlined statement is the **cause**. What is the **effect**?

A. The crayon melted.
B. The crayon floated.
C. The crayon sank.

RSVP

Jerome sent his friends an email inviting them to his graduation party. He asked them to let him know if they were going to attend. Caroline was the first to respond to his email. She said she was looking forward to going to the party.

The underlined statement is the **effect**. What is the **cause**?

A. Jerome invited Caroline to his graduation party.
B. Caroline's mom asked her if she was going.
C. Jerome had to cancel his graduation party.

Homework Helper

Annabelle didn't understand her math homework. She had been out sick from school for the past two days. She had missed the math lesson about multiplying fractions. Annabelle went to her neighbor's house to ask for help. Her neighbor Jackson was in her class. Jackson was in class for the math lesson and said he could help Annabelle.

The underlined statement is the **cause**. What is the **effect**?

A. Annabelle didn't get to turn in her math homework.
B. Jackson was in class for the math lesson.
C. Annabelle didn't understand her math homework.

Name _____ **Date** _____

Clean and Shout

Simon was vacuuming the living room carpet. It was difficult to hear anything over the noise of the vacuum. I asked Simon if he needed help. "What?" shouted Simon. I asked again. <u>"I can't hear you!" he shouted.</u> By the time Simon turned off the vacuum, he was all done.

The underlined statement is the **effect**. What is the **cause**?

A. Simon didn't need any help vacuuming.

B. The noise of the vacuum cleaner was too loud.

C. Simon was vacuuming the living room carpet.

Perilous Plunge

"Perilous Plunge" is the name of the new water slide at the water park. It looked scary, but I didn't want my friends to see that I was nervous. As we climbed the stairs to the top, <u>I told my friends that I couldn't ride because I had a stomachache.</u> They didn't believe me. Then my friends said, "We were nervous the first time, too. When you get to the bottom, you will want to go again!"

The underlined statement is the **cause**. What is the **effect**?

A. My friends and I climbed up the stairs.

B. My friends went on the water slide with me again.

C. My friends didn't believe me.

Finding a Home for the President

The capital of the United States is in Washington, D.C. The White House is also in Washington, D.C. The White House is where the president lives. <u>George Washington was the first president of the United States, but he did not live in the White House.</u> He was, however, the person who chose where the new capital would be. It took many years to build a new capital city and a house for the president.

The underlined statement is the **effect**. What is the **cause**?

A. The capital of the United States is in Washington, D.C.

B. The White House was not yet built when George Washington was president.

C. George Washington didn't want the capital to be Washington, D.C.

Name _____ **Date** _____

Squeaky Steps

Joseph's right shoe made a squeaking sound with every step he took. He was at school, so he couldn't take his shoes off. He walked slowly at recess to avoid hearing too many squeaks. <u>After recess, the squeaking got louder.</u> Joseph's teacher gave him permission to take off his shoe.

The underlined statement is the **cause**. What is the **effect**?

A. Joseph's teacher told him not to wear tennis shoes.
B. Joseph's teacher allowed him to take off his shoe.
C. Joseph's shoe made squeaking sounds when he walked.

Out of the Picture

It was almost the end of the school year. Everyone was excited because the yearbooks were ready. Jasmine flipped through her yearbook and looked at the pictures. <u>She found her class picture, but she was not in it.</u> Jasmine wondered why. Then she remembered that she had been absent from school on picture day.

The underlined statement is the **effect**. What is the **cause**?

A. Jasmine had been absent on picture day.
B. Jasmine didn't want to be in the class picture.
C. Jasmine joined her class in the middle of the school year.

Freeze Tag

The neighborhood children love to play freeze tag after school. <u>Yesterday, Mara was "it" and tagged Janet.</u> Janet had to stand still and be "frozen." The other players tried to "unfreeze" Janet by tagging her. Many of them got tagged by Mara before they reached Janet.

The underlined statement is the **cause**. What is the **effect**?

A. Janet had to "freeze" by standing still.
B. The children love to play freeze tag after school.
C. Janet tried to "unfreeze" the other players.

Name _____ **Date** _____

Swinging by the Hospital

Nicholas fell off the swing set in his uncle's back yard and landed on his arm. He was in a lot of pain, and Nicholas thought he had broken his arm. <u>Nicholas's parents drove him to the hospital emergency room.</u> The x-rays showed that his arm was not broken.

The underlined statement is the **effect**. What is the **cause**?

A. Nicholas thought his arm was broken.

B. Nicholas was in pain and had no idea why.

C. The x-rays showed that Nicholas's arm was not broken.

Candle Complications

Audrey saw the candle flickering from a distance. <u>She blew really hard to put out the flame</u>, but nothing happened. "What is wrong with this candle?" asked Audrey in frustration. "It's an electric candle," said her mother, laughing. "Turn the switch off at the bottom."

The underlined statement is the **cause**. What is the **effect**?

A. The candle burned Audrey's finger.

B. Audrey wanted to blow out the candle.

C. The candle could not be blown out.

Solve the Riddle

Pete asked his friend Olivia to solve a riddle. He said, "Mary's father has four children. Three are named Nana, Nene, and Nini. What is the fourth child's name?" Olivia was going to answer "Nono," but then she stopped herself. She thought carefully about what Pete said. Then she came up with the correct answer. <u>"The fourth child's name is Mary," she said with a smile.</u>

The underlined statement is the **effect**. What is the **cause**?

A. Olivia knew that the next vowel was "o."

B. Olivia thought carefully about what Pete had said.

C. Olivia asked Pete to repeat the riddle.

Name _____ Date _____

Late-Night Gaming

Enrique bought a new video game with some money he had earned from helping his neighbors. <u>He stayed up three hours past his bedtime playing the new game along with his older brother.</u> The next day, Enrique was very tired. He was regretting not getting enough sleep.

The underlined statement is the **cause**. What is the **effect**?

A. Enrique was very tired.
B. Enrique bought a new game.
C. Enrique went to bed early.

One More Canary

The magician at the school carnival was amazing. I still don't understand how he did his first trick. There were two canaries in a cage. The magician covered the birdcage with a blanket. When he lifted up the blanket, a third canary had appeared. <u>The audience clapped and cheered.</u>

The underlined statement is the **effect**. What is the **cause**?

A. There were two canaries inside the cage.
B. Another bird appeared inside the cage.
C. The magician covered the cage with a blanket.

Water Hazard

There was a lot of water on the kitchen floor. <u>Someone had knocked over a water glass.</u> Bernadette quickly grabbed a towel and cleaned up the spill. She didn't want anyone to accidentally slip and fall.

The underlined statement is the **cause**. What is the **effect**?

A. Bernadette slipped and fell.
B. The water glass broke.
C. There was water on the floor.

Name _____ **Date** _____

No Peeking!

Aaron and Tara took a typing class last November. The teacher told the class to avoid looking at their keyboards while they type. Aaron and Tara did not listen. <u>Now they struggle with typing whenever they look away from the keys.</u> Both of them signed up for another typing class.

The underlined statement is the **effect**. What is the **cause**?

- **A.** Aaron and Tara took a typing class last November.
- **B.** Aaron and Tara didn't listen to the directions.
- **C.** Aaron and Tara wanted to take the typing class again.

Insert Another Quarter

Eli's dad took him to the arcade. Eli put his quarter into one of the video-game machines. He pressed the start button, but nothing happened. <u>The machine said to insert another quarter.</u> Eli put in another quarter and had fun playing the game.

The underlined statement is the **cause**. What is the **effect**?

- **A.** Eli's dad took him to the arcade.
- **B.** Eli put in another quarter.
- **C.** Eli put a quarter into the machine and pressed the start button.

Hard-Earned Money

Ryan earns money by doing work after school. He gets three dollars for every job he does. Yesterday, Ryan mowed the neighbor's lawn, took out her trash, and raked his grandmother's yard. <u>He earned nine dollars</u> and used some of the money to buy a smoothie and a magazine.

The underlined statement is the **effect**. What is the **cause**?

- **A.** Ryan completed three jobs.
- **B.** Ryan bought a smoothie and a magazine.
- **C.** Ryan raked his grandmother's yard.

Name _____ Date _____

Koala (Not) Bears

Koala bears live in Australia. Contrary to popular belief, they are not bears. They are marsupials. Marsupials are mammals with pouches. Koalas spend eighteen to twenty hours each day sleeping. Koalas only eat eucalyptus leaves. They can eat one to fifteen pounds of leaves a day. The leaves don't have a lot of calories. <u>They don't provide a koala with much energy.</u> Sleeping helps a koala conserve energy.

The underlined statement is the **cause**. What is the **effect**?

 A. A koala is a marsupial.
 B. A koala only eats eucalyptus leaves.
 C. A koala conserves energy by sleeping a lot.

Canned-Vegetable Garden

Tyler and his little sister Dana were planting vegetables in their garden. Tyler decided to dig up the ground a bit more where Dana had already dug because he knew the seeds would grow better if planted in soft dirt. <u>Tyler's shovel hit something hard.</u> He dug up a can of green beans. "Dana!" cried Tyler. "That's not how you plant vegetables!"

The underlined statement is the **effect**. What is the **cause**?

 A. Seeds grow better if planted in soft dirt.
 B. Dana buried a can of green beans in the garden.
 C. Tyler and his sister enjoyed eating vegetables.

Change of Plans

Every year my family goes on a camping trip. This year we had to cancel our trip. <u>There were big thunderstorms at the campsite.</u> It rained so hard that the river overflooded its banks. It was not safe to go. My parents said we could camp out in our back yard instead. We even roasted marshmallows over the barbecue grill.

The underlined statement is the **cause**. What is the **effect**?

 A. We had to cancel our trip.
 B. We wanted to camp in the back yard instead.
 C. The campsite we use is by a river.

Name _____ **Date** _____

Morning Visitor

Someone knocked on our front door at 7:00 this morning. They must have left right away. <u>I immediately got out of bed</u> when I heard the knocking. When I looked through the peephole, I didn't see anyone standing outside.

The underlined statement is the **effect**. What is the **cause**?

A. Someone looked through the peephole.

B. I didn't see anyone standing outside.

C. Someone knocked on the front door.

Two Right Answers?

Claire said there are only eleven letters in the alphabet. Owen said there are 26 letters in the alphabet. Owen said, "We can't both be right. I counted all the letters from A to Z, and I got 26, so I know I am right." Then Claire knew they were both right. <u>They had counted different things.</u> Owen had counted the number of letters in the alphabet, but Claire had counted the total number of letters in the words "the alphabet."

The underlined statement is the **cause**. What is the **effect**?

A. They were both right.

B. Owen was right because there are 26 letters in the alphabet.

C. Claire and Owen disagree about a lot of things.

Way Too Heavy

The bowling game was about to begin. Isaiah thought all bowling balls were light and weighed the same. He started to pick up a ball he thought weighed eight pounds. The ball weighed sixteen pounds! <u>Isaiah struggled when picking up the ball and dropped it a couple seconds later.</u>

The underlined statement is the **effect**. What is the **cause**?

A. Isaiah didn't know how to hold the bowling ball.

B. The bowling ball weighed eight pounds.

C. The bowling ball was too heavy for Isaiah.

Name _____ **Date** _____

Morning Routine

1. Lana's alarm clock woke her up at 6:30 in the morning.

2. Lana rode her bike and got to school ten minutes early.

3. She then got dressed and ate a healthy breakfast.

4. The first thing Lana did was go to the bathroom to brush her teeth.

What is the correct sequence?

A. 1, 4, 3, 2

B. 2, 3, 1, 4

C. 4, 2, 3, 1

Good Citizen

1. A man who also was looking at stoves picked up the purse and gave it back to Ms. Moon.

2. She put her purse down on the floor while she looked at a white stove.

3. Ms. Moon was shopping for a new stove.

4. She accidentally forgot about her purse when she went to look for a sales clerk.

Which sentence comes first?

A. Sentence 1

B. Sentence 2

C. Sentence 3

Name _____ **Date** _____

Color Change

1. The teacher filled a clear glass up with water.

2. He placed a white flower that had a long, freshly-cut stem into the blue water.

3. He added twenty drops of blue food coloring to the water.

4. The next day, the white flower petals had turned blue.

What is the correct sequence?

  A. 4, 2, 3, 1

  B. 1, 3, 2, 4

  C. 1, 4, 3, 2

Helping Hands

1. Tom's brother gave him one end of the measuring tape and held on to the other end.

2. Tom stretched the measuring tape to the edge of the table, and his brother noted that it was six feet two inches long.

3. Tom's brother asked, "Will you help me measure the kitchen table?"

4. Tom replied, "Sure. I'll help you hold the measuring tape."

Which sentence comes third?

  A. Sentence 3

  B. Sentence 1

  C. Sentence 4

Name _____ **Date** _____

Fall Colors

1. She wondered why some of the leaves looked orange.

2. The girl was painting a picture of a tree blossoming in the fall.

3. Then she remembered that when red and yellow are mixed together, they make orange.

4. She painted some red leaves on the tree close to some yellow leaves.

What is the correct sequence?
  A. 4, 1, 3, 2
  B. 2, 3, 1, 4
  C. 2, 4, 1, 3

Sailing East

1. After leaving California, they headed over Nevada.

2. Brent and Bree sailed across the United States in a hot-air balloon.

3. The sun on the Atlantic Ocean was a sight to see.

4. They started on the West Coast and went east.

Which sentence comes second?
  A. Sentence 1
  B. Sentence 3
  C. Sentence 4

Name _____ **Date** _____

Candy Math

1. In the bag, Hope counted sixteen pieces of candy.

2. Hope divided sixteen by four to see how many candies each friend would get.

3. Hope figured out that they could each eat four pieces of candy.

4. Hope bought a bag of sour candies to share with three friends.

What is the correct sequence?
  A. 4, 1, 2, 3
  B. 4, 2, 1, 3
  C. 4, 3, 2, 1

Alphabet Assessment

1. Jamaal got called up to the board to put some words in alphabetical order.

2. Right away, Jamaal noticed that all four words started with the letters *ch*.

3. Jamaal read the words *chair, chicken, cheese,* and *chug*.

4. He knew to look at the third letter in each word to put them in the correct order.

Which sentence comes first?
  A. Sentence 1
  B. Sentence 4
  C. Sentence 2

Name _____ **Date** _____

Summer Fun

1. The boy's mom put on sunscreen while she watched her son swim.

2. She jumped into the pool afterwards because she felt hot.

3. After the sunscreen dried, the boy dove into his backyard pool.

4. It was a warm day, so the boy changed into his bathing suit and then put on sunscreen.

What is the correct sequence?

A. 1, 4, 2, 3

B. 4, 3, 1, 2

C. 1, 4, 3, 2

Simple Sandwich

1. Then place one slice of bread with a slice of cheese on top in a pan (butter-side down).

2. Cook both sides of the sandwich until each side is golden brown and the cheese has melted.

3. To make a grilled cheese sandwich, first butter two slices of bread.

4. Place the other slice of bread on top of the cheese (butter-side up).

Which sentence comes second?

A. Sentence 2

B. Sentence 3

C. Sentence 1

Name _____ **Date** _____

Party Planner

1. Joy knew that twenty people were coming, so she counted to make sure she had set up the right number of chairs.

2. Joy was planning a surprise party for her sister.

3. On the day of the party, Joy started setting up tables and chairs.

4. She set up five tables with four chairs at each one.

What is the correct sequence?

A. 2, 3, 4, 1
B. 2, 3, 1, 4
C. 3, 2, 4, 1

Recess Romp

1. Recess ended at 10:15 a.m., and we all lined up at the door.

2. After we were done eating, we played handball on the blacktop.

3. During recess, we all ate a snack together on the lunch benches.

4. When it was time for recess, my friends and I grabbed our jackets and went outside.

Which sentence comes third?

A. Sentence 3
B. Sentence 2
C. Sentence 1

Name _____ **Date** _____

A Sinking Feeling

1. Tim immediately took off his backpack.

2. Tim was hiking in Florida, and he stepped into some quicksand.

3. Tim moved very slowly towards the dry land.

4. Tim knew his body was less dense than quicksand, so he couldn't sink unless he struggled too much or was weighed down by something heavy.

What is the correct sequence?

  A. 4, 1, 3, 2

  B. 2, 4, 1, 3

  C. 1, 3, 4, 2

Food List

1. Linda gathered all the items from her list except bean sprouts.

2. After looking for them for a few minutes, Linda asked a store clerk to help her find them.

3. Linda took her list with her to the grocery store.

4. Linda wrote a list of food items she needed to buy from the store.

Which sentence comes last?

  A. Sentence 2

  B. Sentence 3

  C. Sentence 4

Name _____ Date _____

Use Your Head

1. Hugh wanted to protect his brain.

2. When Hugh first started skateboarding, he didn't wear his helmet.

3. Hugh does not start to skateboard until he puts on his helmet.

4. Then Hugh read a story about how even a little fall can be harmful to one's brain.

What is the correct sequence?

   A. 2, 1, 3, 4
   B. 4, 2, 1, 3
   C. 2, 4, 1, 3

A Gift for Mom

1. Wren's mom was very happy when she saw pretty roses sitting on the dining room table.

2. Wren cut five roses from the garden, put them into the glass, and filled it with water.

3. She took her scissors and a clear drinking glass to the back yard.

4. Wren decided to do something nice for her mom.

Which sentence comes first?

   A. Sentence 3
   B. Sentence 1
   C. Sentence 4

Name _____   **Date** _____

It's a Riddle

1. Sydney thought about what could happen twice in a week, once in a year, but never in a day.

2. Sydney laughed when she found it was the letter "e."

3. Sydney told Brett that there was not an answer to what he asked.

4. Brett asked Sydney, "What happens twice in a week, once in a year, but never in a day?"

What is the correct sequence?

  A. 4, 1, 3, 2
  B. 1, 4, 2, 3
  C. 3, 1, 4, 2

Pizza Delivery

1. Ron's dad thought pizza was a great idea and asked Ron what kind he wanted.

2. Ron's dad called the pizza parlor and ordered two pizzas to be delivered.

3. Ron was so hungry when the pizza arrived that he ate five slices!

4. Ron was getting hungry, so he asked his dad if they could order pizza for dinner.

Which sentence comes third?

  A. Sentence 1
  B. Sentence 2
  C. Sentence 3

Name _____ **Date** _____

Beginner's Luck

1. Juana joined a bowling league last month that plays every Sunday.

2. During her first bowling game, Juana got a total of four strikes.

3. In her next game, Juana only got one strike.

4. Juana only got two strikes during her final game of the season.

What is the correct sequence?

A. 4, 3, 2, 1

B. 1, 2, 3, 4

C. 3, 1, 2, 4

Goodbye, Flame

1. The candle burned for a few seconds, and then the flame went out.

2. The science teacher put a glass jar over the lit candle.

3. For the experiment, the science teacher lit a candle by using a match.

4. The teacher said that the candle's flame had gone out because all the oxygen inside the jar had been used up.

Which sentence comes last?

A. Sentence 2

B. Sentence 1

C. Sentence 4

Name _____ **Date** _____

Lost in the Zoo

1. They found Nate and Nora looking at the zebras thirty minutes later.

2. The group members looked for Nate and Nora near the monkey exhibit.

3. A few minutes later, Sam and Selena noticed that Nate and Nora were missing.

4. While at the zoo, Nate and Nora left their group without anyone knowing.

What is the correct sequence?

A. 4, 3, 2, 1

B. 4, 2, 1, 3

C. 2, 1, 3, 4

Math Minded

1. To get the right answer, Carlos multiplied 7×6.

2. One of the math problems said to add $7 + 7 + 7 + 7 + 7 + 7$.

3. Instead of adding, Carlos decided it would be faster to multiply.

4. Carlos sat down to finish his math homework.

Which sentence comes third?

A. Sentence 1

B. Sentence 3

C. Sentence 4

Name _____   Date _____

An Important Tail

1. After she read that the Gila monster lives in the desert, she read something interesting about its tail.

2. The Gila monster stores fat in its tail.

3. Zoey borrowed a book from the library about a monster that was really a lizard.

4. When food is scarce, the Gila monster breaks down the fat that is in its tail.

What is the correct sequence?

A. 3, 4, 1, 2

B. 3, 1, 2, 4

C. 3, 2, 4, 1

Barking Loudly

1. When the dog barked at me again, I realized that it may not have heard me, but it saw me!

2. The next day, I walked extra quietly so the dog wouldn't hear me.

3. Two days after that, I gave the dog a toy, and it never barked at me again.

4. Last week, the dog next door barked at me when I walked in front of its house.

Which sentence comes first?

A. Sentence 2

B. Sentence 3

C. Sentence 4

Name _____ **Date** _____

Snow Friend

1. While on winter vacation, Ava wanted to build a snowman.

2. Ava stacked the smaller snowballs on top of the largest one.

3. As a final touch, Ava added sticks for arms and rocks for the eyes and nose.

4. She piled snow together to make three different-sized balls of snow.

What is the correct sequence?

  A. 1, 2, 4, 3

  B. 1, 4, 2, 3

  C. 2, 4, 1, 3

Toddler Television

1. "Thank you," Todd's mother said as she took the remote from Todd.

2. The TV turned on and got louder.

3. Todd grabbed the remote from the toddler and quickly pressed the off button.

4. The toddler got a hold of the TV remote control and pushed random buttons.

Which sentence comes last?

  A. Sentence 4

  B. Sentence 2

  C. Sentence 1

Name _____ **Date** _____

Where Did I Put That?

1. On the morning of the play, Bruce forgot where he had put the costume.

2. Bruce bought his costume a month early.

3. As soon as Bruce brought the costume home, he put it in a bag under his bed.

4. After searching through his closet, he remembered the costume was under his bed.

What is the correct sequence?
   A. 2, 3, 1, 4
   B. 1, 4, 3, 2
   C. 3, 4, 1, 2

Seasonal Spirit

1. On Valentine's Day, Kim wore to school a pair of red pants and a pink shirt.

2. Then in March, on St. Patrick's Day, Kim wore green pants and a green shirt.

3. Kim made a New Year's resolution to dress in holiday colors for each holiday that year.

4. On the Fourth of July, Kim wore a combination of red, white, and blue clothes.

Which sentence comes second?
   A. Sentence 1
   B. Sentence 2
   C. Sentence 3

Name _____ **Date** _____

"Eggciting" Science

1. Bailey said, "I never thought it was possible."

2. Bailey was sure it was impossible.

3. Holden put an egg in a glass of vinegar until the shell dissolved, and the egg was only held together by a soft membrane.

4. Holden told Bailey he could remove the shell of an egg without cracking it.

What is the correct sequence?

A. 4, 1, 3, 2
B. 1, 2, 3, 4
C. 4, 2, 3, 1

Campaign Trail

1. Later that week, Han gave a speech about why his peers should vote for him.

2. Han decided to run for fourth-grade president.

3. He started by making signs that said "Vote for Han" and hanging them around the school.

4. Han felt proud when he won the election and became the fourth-grade president.

Which sentence comes third?

A. Sentence 1
B. Sentence 2
C. Sentence 3

Name _____ **Date** _____

Under Pressure

Manuel looked at the timer and started to panic. "Eight more problems left to do in only two minutes. I wish I had more time," Manuel thought. "Well, if four friends are sharing sixteen sour candies, each friend will get four candies. That wasn't very hard. I just need to focus." Manuel finished the last problem seven seconds before the timer beeped. When the person at the front of the room told everyone to put their pencils down and sit quietly, Manuel was finally able to relax.

Most likely, **what** is Manuel doing?

A. taking a timed math test

B. seeing how long it takes to do his math homework

C. trying out for the school spelling bee

Road Trip

Jeremy, Dawn, and two of their friends went on a road trip with Jeremy and Dawn's parents. After three hours, Jeremy and Dawn's father parked the car. There were tall trees all around. A stream could be heard bubbling behind the trees. The four children helped unload the supplies and food from the car. "Put everything over there," said Jeremy and Dawn's mother.

Most likely, **where** are they?

A. at a hotel

B. at a slumber party

C. at a campsite

Name _____ **Date** _____

Feeling like a New Man

Kevin sat down in the chair and looked at himself in the mirror. A lady was standing behind him. First, she placed a cover around Kevin and made it snug around his neck. Next, she plugged in a small, noisy machine and used it on the back of Kevin's head and around his ears. Then, she used a pair of scissors. When she was all finished, Kevin really liked how he looked.

Most likely, **where** is Kevin?

- **A.** at an art studio
- **B.** at a hair salon
- **C.** at the doctor's office

Island Dream

Kelly dreamed that she was stranded on a deserted island. She didn't have a calendar with her, but she wanted to keep track of how long she was there. Kelly made a scratch in a tree for each passing day. So far, she had made twelve scratches in the tree. She was very hungry, thirsty, and lonely. Suddenly, Kelly woke up and realized that it was all just a bad dream.

Most likely, **how long** was Kelly stranded on the island?

- **A.** twelve days
- **B.** eleven days
- **C.** two weeks

Name _____   **Date** _____

Safe Swimmer

Cynthia took swimming lessons during the summers when she was five and six years old. Now she's seven and still doesn't do well at swimming lessons. She doesn't like her lessons because the water is always cold. One day, Cynthia was at a pool party. The pool was heated so that it felt like a bath. Cynthia's dad noticed that she was swimming much better. "I think we solved the mystery," he said.

Most likely, **why** was Cynthia swimming better?

A. She finally listened to what her swim teacher said.
B. She was more comfortable swimming in warm water.
C. She was wearing a life jacket in the pool.

Ask an Engineer

People like to make gingerbread houses. They decorate the houses with candy. Often, the houses fall apart because the sides collapse or the roof falls in. A civil engineer was asked for advice. Civil engineers build things like roads, bridges, and dams. The engineer said to keep the corners square and to keep everything nice and straight. He said the most important thing was the glue. People often use icing, but icing can be too runny or too stiff. The engineer said to make an edible glue. How does one make glue one can eat? The trick is melting together marshmallows, caramels, and gummy candies. The engineer said that when they are melted, ". . . they become a really strong, cement-like substance."

Most likely, **why** was a civil engineer asked for advice?

A. He knows how to build things that don't fall apart.
B. He has a job building gingerbread houses.
C. He uses cement when building bridges or dams.

Name _____ **Date** _____

Man in Black . . . and White

The Jaguars were playing against the Tigers in the championship game. The score was very close; the Tigers were only down by three points. Ethan, from the Tigers team, had the ball and tried to shoot it, but Justin hit Ethan's arm in mid-shot. A man dressed in black and white blew the whistle. "Foul!" he shouted. Justin was upset by the call, but he knew the man was just enforcing the rules.

Most likely, **who** is the man?

A. the coach of the Tigers
B. Justin's dad
C. the referee

Cup of Pellets

Taylor bought a cup of pellets that she knew animals would enjoy eating. She gave a small handful to the first goat she saw. It licked the food right out of her hands. When she saw how many animals there were all around, Taylor decided to only give out a few pellets at a time. Taylor felt a sheep's soft wool. She even got to brush a miniature horse's hair.

Most likely, **where** is Taylor?

A. in the jungle
B. at a petting zoo
C. at a pet store

Name _____ **Date** _____

Familiar Friends

When Gwen looks through the fence in her back yard, she can sometimes see Martin playing in his back yard. One time, Gwen accidentally hit a tennis ball into Martin's back yard. Martin was kind enough to throw it back over to her. Martin and Gwen are such good friends that they wish they went to the same school.

Most likely, **how** do Gwen and Martin know each other?

A. They are neighbors.
B. They are in the same class.
C. They are on the same tennis team.

Unwelcome Surprise

"Oh, no!" shouted Derrick as he walked into the bathroom. "There's water everywhere!" Derrick's dad came rushing into the bathroom. Neither one of them knew where the water was coming from. Derrick's dad decided to call someone who could help. Soon, a man named Mr. Thomas arrived with several tools. After looking at the pipes in the bathroom, Mr. Thomas said he found a leak in one of the pipes. He told Derrick's dad that he could fix it.

Most likely, **who** is Mr. Thomas?

A. a cleaner
B. a builder
C. a plumber

Name _____ Date _____

In Costume

Everyone in the fourth grade had practiced for the class play. On the night of the show, the students dressed in their costumes and were ready to perform. Heather was dressed in all gray with a white spot on her belly. She colored her nose pink and put on a headband with floppy ears. She had a fuzzy tail pinned on her. Heather hopped out on stage to open the show.

Most likely, **what** is Heather's costume?

A. a cat

B. a mouse

C. a rabbit

Snow Scenes

What artist sometimes walks for ten hours while making a picture? Simon Beck is an English artist who doesn't use paper. Instead, he uses white snow as his canvas high up in the French Alps. Wearing snow shoes, Beck walks up and down the sides of mountains. He walks carefully, using his tracks to make beautiful patterns on the steep slopes. What does Beck say about his huge pictures? He says, "The mountains improve the artwork, and the artwork improves the mountains."

Most likely, **why** does Beck create his pictures high in the French Alps?

A. so that people can see the pictures in a gallery

B. because there is snow present for much of the year

C. so that he can plan out where he will walk beforehand

Name _____ Date _____

Book Batteries

Lizzie told Greg that she had brought a book called *Press and Listen USA* to show to their teacher. Lizzie's mom bought it for her to help with her social studies homework. Every page has a different map on it. Greg thought the book sounded interesting. He asked Lizzie if he could borrow it. Lizzie said he could, but the book's batteries might need to be replaced.

Most likely, **why** does the book need batteries?

   A. It says state names when you press the states.
   B. It lights up where the capitals are when you press the states.
   C. It lights up the state names when you press the states.

Tomato Twins

Yolanda and her twin brother, Ned, planted a garden in their yard. They started with four tiny tomato plants because they love to eat tomatoes. Ned asked Yolanda if she wanted to have a contest. "The next tomato we eat has to be from our garden. Let's see if we can wait that long," he said. Eventually, they picked their first homegrown tomato. They cut the tomato in half and each took a bite. When Yolanda tasted the tomato, she told Ned that it was worth the wait.

Most likely, **how long** did Ned and Yolanda wait to eat tomatoes?

   A. two days
   B. two months
   C. two years

Name _____ **Date** _____

A Little Extra Help

Mr. Flora goes to the Merced family's house every Monday afternoon. He goes straight to their back yard and gets to work. He mows the lawn and trims the bushes. Sometimes, the grass clippings get into the swimming pool. Mr. Flora always makes sure to clean the grass clippings from the pool. Mrs. Merced asks Mr. Flora to trim the orange trees every year.

Most likely, **who** is Mr. Flora?

A. a gardener

B. a pool cleaner

C. a farmer

Digging Up Trouble

Mr. Tran's dog, Percy, ran into the back yard with something in his mouth and started digging a hole in the yard. "Percy must be burying his dog treat," thought Mr. Tran. Later, Mrs. Tran came home and asked Mr. Tran why he never responded to her text messages. "I never got them. I didn't even hear the beeps," he told his wife. Mr. Tran walked out to where Percy had been digging and heard a beeping sound. "Looks like Percy didn't bury a treat after all," he said angrily.

Most likely, **what** did Percy bury?

A. a toy

B. a phone

C. a watch

Name _____ **Date** _____

Fruit Exchange

At lunchtime, Austin, Dallas, and Phoenix all sat at the same table. Dallas asked Austin if he wanted to trade his banana for orange slices. "No, thanks. I don't like oranges," said Austin. Phoenix asked Austin if he wanted to trade his banana for a small bunch of grapes. Austin thought for a second and decided to make the trade.

Most likely, **why** did Austin trade his banana for grapes?

   A. Austin is allergic to bananas.
   B. Austin wanted to make his friends happy.
   C. Austin likes grapes more than bananas.

Pikes Peak

Ruth is going to visit the state of Colorado. She is excited because her family is going to go to the top of Pikes Peak. Pikes Peak is over 14,000 feet high. It is the easternmost 14,000-foot-high peak in the United States. Ruth's family is planning to drive up the mountain in a car. They will have to drive slowly because the road is so steep. It has lots of switchbacks. Ruth said, "We might not make it to the top. We might have to turn back because of snow. Pikes Peak is so high that snow is possible all year round."

Most likely, **where** is Pikes Peak?

   A. in the Andes Mountains
   B. in the Himalayan Mountains
   C. in the Rocky Mountains

Name _____   Date _____

Easy Money

On a funny game show, a man and a woman stood in a small room with lots and lots of twenty-dollar bills flying around them. Whoever collected the most money would get to keep it. The only thing in the room besides the people and the money was a bottle of maple syrup. The man covered his arms with the syrup. He stuck out his arms and spun around in circles. The woman didn't want to be sticky. She just used her hands to catch the money.

Most likely, **why** did the man cover his arms in syrup?

  A. so the money would stick to him

  B. to be funny on television

  C. the game show host told him to

Morning Exercise

Wayne and Raina live about one mile away from their school, and they walk there every day. It takes them about 20 minutes. This morning, Wayne and Raina took longer than usual to get ready for school. They decided to run to school because they were worried about being late. Wayne and Raina ran the entire way to school, only stopping before crossing busy intersections. When they got to school, they went directly to the drinking fountain.

Most likely, **how long** did it take Wayne and Raina to run to school?

  A. 12 minutes

  B. 20 minutes

  C. 22 minutes

Name _____ **Date** _____

No Hands

Jimmy's mom dropped him off at the park, and he ran out to the field. Jimmy said hello to his friends and to Mr. Willow. Mr. Willow blew his whistle and told everyone to run around and kick a ball. Then, one by one, all the kids practiced kicking a ball into a goal. Mr. Willow told Jimmy that he is not allowed to touch the ball with his hands.

Most likely, **who** is Mr. Willow?

   A. Jimmy's fourth-grade teacher

   B. Jimmy's best friend

   C. Jimmy's soccer coach

All Shook Up

Cassie's daughter Alyssa moved to a different state to go to college. Cassie and Alyssa often talked to each other on the phone. They sent text messages, too, to keep in touch. One day, Alyssa was watching the news. She saw that there had been an earthquake in her mom's city. Alyssa called her mom right away. "The bookshelf fell over and some dishes broke, but I'm okay," her mom said. "Fortunately, the Christmas tree didn't fall over, but it was leaning to one side!" Alyssa was happy that her mom was not hurt.

Most likely, **when** was the earthquake?

   A. October 4

   B. December 20

   C. January 31

Name _____ **Date** _____

Lights Out

Everyone crowded into the room, and Dad turned off the lights. Mom came in carrying something with nine lit candles on it. We all started singing as soon as we saw the candles. Jessica blew out the candles when the song was over, and then we clapped for her. Then Mom turned the lights back on and gave everyone something to eat.

Most likely, **what** was Jessica's mom carrying?

  A. a birthday cake

  B. a present

  C. a candle holder

Foggy Surprise

Lance moved to the coast. He had never lived by the ocean before. Lance was not surprised when the air smelled salty, but he was surprised at the fog. One day, the fog was so dense that his school day was delayed for two hours. Lance heard on the news that most school days along the eastern seaboard were also delayed.

Most likely, **where** did Lance move?

  A. New Mexico

  B. Oregon

  C. Maine

Mouse Madness

Misty always follows Rachel around and wants to play. One day, Misty and Rachel were in the back yard. Suddenly, Misty was distracted by a mouse that ran by. She ran after the mouse and tried to catch it. Rachel was amazed at how fast Misty could run! Misty must have been tired after the big chase because she curled up and took a nap.

Most likely, **who** is Misty?

  A. Rachel's sister
  B. Rachel's friend
  C. Rachel's cat

Quarter Races

It was very noisy in the room. Jeff put a five-dollar bill into a machine, and it gave him twenty quarters. He used the quarters to play the games. For some games, he only needed one quarter to play, but for other games, he needed two quarters. Jeff's favorite game was the one where he drives a racecar around a track.

Most likely, **where** is Jeff?

  A. at a video-game store
  B. at an arcade
  C. at a racecar track

Name _____ **Date** _____

A Fancy Invitation

Dylan and Linny received a fancy invitation in the mail. The invitation said to go to the Green Hills Golf Course. Dylan and Linny dressed in nice clothes and drove to the golf course. They didn't see their friend Daisy when they arrived, but they sat down anyway. Shortly after they sat down, Daisy walked right past them. Daisy was wearing a beautiful, white dress. She was carrying a bouquet of roses.

Most likely, **why** did Dylan and Linny go to the golf course?

A. They went to play golf with Daisy.

B. They went to see Daisy's wedding.

C. They went to help Daisy prune the rose bushes.

Well-Prepared

The students were busily working at their desks when the bell rang. "Everyone, go outside without running or pushing," said the teacher. Everyone in the entire school quickly walked out of the buildings and gathered on the grass field. Eight minutes later, they all returned to their classrooms. "Great job," said the teacher. "You are all well-prepared."

Most likely, **why** did everyone go outside?

A. They were having a fire drill.

B. It was recess time.

C. School was over for the day.

Name _____ **Date** _____

Delayed Dinner

Brian wasn't ready for dinner at the same time as the rest of his family. His mother told Brian he could eat later. By the time Brian was ready, his food had gotten cold. Brian pressed the one-minute button to warm up his food. After that, the food was just the right temperature. Brian enjoyed his dinner, even though he had to eat it by himself.

Most likely, **how** did Brian warm up his food?

A. in the oven
B. on the stove
C. in the microwave

Two-Headed Snake

A two-headed snake was brought to a zoo. People came from all over to see the unusual sight. Herpetologists study snakes. The herpetologist at the zoo said that the snake was lucky to have been found. He said that it didn't have a chance of surviving in the wild. The two heads would fight over what direction to go. They might not want to hunt at the same time. If they did catch something, they would fight over which head would eat it.

Most likely, **why** were people so interested in seeing a two-headed snake?

A. They grow quicker than other snakes.
B. They are rare.
C. They eat more than other snakes.

Name _____ **Date** _____

Pool Party

Pam needs eyeglasses to help her see well. Pam wears glasses every day. She only takes her glasses off when she is sleeping or in water. Pam used to wear contact lenses, but she did not like the way they felt. She doesn't wear them anymore. Her new glasses are stylish, and she likes the way they look on her. Pam is going to a pool party tomorrow.

Predict the outcome.

   A. Pam will take off her eyeglasses when she goes swimming.
   B. Pam will wear contact lenses in the pool.
   C. Pam will not wear eyeglasses all weekend.

Dollar Scoops

The ice-cream shop near Ray's house sells each scoop of ice cream or sorbet for a dollar. It is selling scoops of lemon sorbet and chocolate chip ice cream. Ray is going to the ice-cream shop today. He has a few dollars in his pocket. Ray really likes chocolate, but he thinks the lemon flavor is too sour.

Predict the outcome.

   A. Ray will buy some lemon sorbet.
   B. Ray will buy one scoop of each flavor.
   C. Ray will buy some chocolate chip ice cream.

Name _____   **Date** _____

Pay to Play

A ticket is required to play the games or to go on the rides at the carnival. Each ticket costs fifty cents. Carnival games cost either one, two, or three tickets each. All rides cost four tickets each. The balloon-popping dart game only costs one ticket. Anthony played that game several times. Anthony is now waiting in line to ride on the Ferris wheel.

Predict the outcome.

  A. Anthony will pay for his ride with one ticket.
  B. Anthony will pay for his ride with three tickets.
  C. Anthony will pay for his ride with four tickets.

Blue Glue

Renee told her mom that she was all out of glue for her craft projects. While Renee's mom was at the store, she saw purple and blue school glue. Renee's mom read the label on the bottle of blue glue, and then she bought it. Renee didn't want the glue to be blue for her crafts, but Renee's mom told her that the glue will be clear when it dries. Renee used the glue and waited for it to dry.

Predict the outcome.

  A. The glue will be purple when it dries.
  B. The glue will be clear when it dries.
  C. The glue will be blue when it dries.

Name _____ Date _____

No Recipe Required

One day last week, Roberto didn't eat lunch at school. He was very hungry when he got home that afternoon. He thought about what he could make to eat. Roberto took out two slices of wheat bread from the cupboard. Next, he gathered turkey slices, cheese, pickles, and mustard from the refrigerator.

Predict the outcome.

A. Roberto will make and eat a sandwich.

B. Roberto will write a recipe for making a sandwich.

C. Roberto will pack his school lunch.

Tilted Axis

Earth's axis is tilted. For six months of the year, the Northern Hemisphere is tilted toward the Sun. The Southern Hemisphere is tilted away from the Sun. For the other six months, it is the opposite: the Northern Hemisphere is tilting away from the Sun, and the Southern Hemisphere is tilting toward the Sun. The part of Earth tilting toward the Sun is warmer. It will be spring and summer there. It will be fall and winter on the part of Earth tilting away from the Sun. Gavin and Addison live in the United States. They live in the Northern Hemisphere. In February, they will leave the Northern Hemisphere. They will go to Australia.

Predict the outcome.

A. Gavin and Addison will be cold once they get to Australia.

B. Gavin and Addison will be warm once they get to Australia.

C. Gavin and Addison will go to where Earth is tilting away from the Sun.

Name _____ **Date** _____

Animal Acrobatics

Landon was walking on a trail. Suddenly, he saw a small animal in front of him. The animal looked like a skunk, but it had black and white spots instead of stripes. When Landon went to look closer, the animal did a handstand! That was when Landon wondered if what he was seeing was a spotted skunk. Spotted skunks will warn predators that they are about to spray by first doing a handstand.

Predict the outcome.

A. Landon will scare the animal away by making a loud noise.
B. Landon will slowly back away from the animal.
C. Landon will try to catch the animal.

Peanuts and Sprinkles

Gregory and Natalie went to an ice-cream shop with their mother. Their mom said they could each order one scoop of ice cream and one topping. The ice-cream shop only had two toppings left—peanuts and sprinkles. Gregory is allergic to peanuts.

Predict the outcome.

A. Gregory will order sprinkles.
B. Gregory will order peanuts.
C. Gregory will order both toppings.

Rover

While Casey was walking home, she read a sign on a tree about a lost dog named "Rover." The sign said that if the dog is found and returned to the owner, a $200 reward will be given. The picture on the sign showed a white dog with brown spots. The next day, Casey saw a dog walking by itself. She looked at the dog's collar and the tag said "Rover." Casey called the phone number from the sign.

Predict the outcome.

A. Casey will earn $200 for walking dogs.

B. Casey will pay $200 to keep the dog as her pet.

C. Casey will return the dog and get $200.

Family Bowl

Bowling is the Robinson family's favorite sport. They go bowling together about once a month. One day, Mr. Robinson received a bowling coupon in the mail. It read, "Buy two games, get one game free." That night, Mr. Robinson took his son and his daughter bowling. He was going to buy just one game for them, but then he decided to buy two.

Predict the outcome.

A. Mr. Robinson will get a higher score than his children.

B. The Robinsons will get a gift card to go bowling.

C. The Robinsons will get an extra game of bowling for free.

Name _____ **Date** _____

April Showers

Kendra was walking home from the library. Usually, it takes her 20 minutes to get home. Kendra carried her books in her backpack. Her backpack was made of waterproof materials. A few minutes after leaving the library, it started to rain. Kendra wished she had an umbrella with her.

Predict the outcome.

   A. Kendra's books will get wet.
   B. Kendra will check out more books.
   C. Kendra will get very wet.

Planetary Positions

Chase was excited. There was going to be an eclipse that day. Chase said, "A lunar eclipse is when Earth passes between the Moon and the Sun. Earth's shadow hides all or part of the Moon. A solar eclipse is when the Moon passes between Earth and the Sun. The Moon blocks all or part of the Sun. Today the sky will darken even though the Sun will be high in the sky. The Moon will be blocking the sunlight."

Predict the outcome.

   A. Chase will see the effect of a lunar eclipse.
   B. Chase will see the effect of a solar eclipse.
   C. Chase will see Earth's shadow hide the Moon.

Candles on the Cake

Mrs. Knott went to the bakery to buy a birthday cake for her daughter. She asked the man to write "Happy 9th Birthday, Abby" on the cake. Abby's friends came over later that day for her birthday party. Mrs. Knott asked one of Abby's friends to put the candles on the cake.

Predict the outcome.

A. The friend will put eight candles on the cake.
B. The friend will put nine candles on the cake.
C. The friend will put eleven candles on the cake.

Clean-O

Isaac's mom bought new laundry detergent called "Clean-O." She used it to wash Isaac's clothes. Later that day, Isaac wore a shirt from the newly-washed pile of clothes. A few minutes later, Isaac began to itch all over. Isaac grabbed a different shirt from the clean pile and changed his shirt. He was still itchy. Finally, Isaac changed into a shirt that had been washed using a different detergent. Isaac stopped itching. He must be allergic to the new detergent.

Predict the outcome.

A. Isaac's mom will no longer wash his clothes with Clean-O.
B. Isaac's mom will keep washing his clothes with Clean-O.
C. Isaac's mom will buy Isaac some new shirts to wear.

Name _____ **Date** _____

For Emergency Use Only

Madelyn's parents gave her a cell phone to use in case of an emergency. The phone plan only allows the phone to be used for 120 minutes each month. Texting is not allowed. If she texts anyone or talks for too many minutes, her parents will have to pay more on the bill. The first month Madelyn had the phone, she didn't use it at all.

Predict the outcome.

   A. Madelyn's parents will not be billed for extra charges.

   B. Madelyn will send text messages to her friends.

   C. Madelyn will have to pay the phone bill.

Costume Party

John's birthday is on October 30, the day before Halloween. Every year, he asks his friends to wear costumes to his birthday party. John says they don't have to, but people in costume will be given their piece of cake first. Kayla and Blake were the first to arrive at John's party. Kayla was wearing a costume, but Blake was not.

Predict the outcome.

   A. Blake will get cake before Kayla.

   B. Kayla will get cake before Blake.

   C. Blake will not be allowed to eat cake.

Name _____ Date _____

Cans for Cash

Bernard and Leah collect aluminum cans. When Bernard and Leah have saved a lot, they take the cans down to a recycling center. The cans are put onto a scale. Each pound of cans is worth a certain amount of money. Bernard and Leah always take the money they get, and they put it in a special piggy bank. When the piggy bank is full, Bernard and Leah take the money to the local bank. Last night, Bernard and Leah couldn't fit any more money into their piggy bank.

Predict the outcome.

A. Bernard and Leah will no longer collect aluminum cans.
B. Bernard and Leah will start keeping their money in a different piggy bank.
C. Bernard and Leah will take their money to a local bank.

"Bloodshot" Eyes

Some horned lizards have a very strange defense. They squirt blood from their eyes! They can shoot the blood almost fifty inches! How much blood can a horned lizard shoot? They can shoot up to one-third of their blood! Usually, squirting blood is a horned lizard's last defense. First, a horned lizard will try to scare away predators by puffing itself up so that it looks bigger. If that doesn't work, it will jump forward and hiss. While hiking last summer, Micah and Christy saw a horned lizard and a snake. Christy said, "Did you hear that? The horned lizard is hissing!"

Predict the outcome.

A. The horned lizard will squirt blood from its eyes.
B. The horned lizard will puff itself up.
C. The horned lizard will jump backwards.

Name _____ **Date** _____

Morning Beeps

Don uses an alarm clock to wake himself up in the morning. When Don sets his alarm, he can choose to have it make one of several different sounds. The alarm can be set to the sound of ocean waves, birds chirping, or just a simple beeping sound. Don tried setting his alarm to both the sound of birds chirping and ocean waves, but he did not wake up to those sounds. Only the beeping sound wakes him up right away.

Predict the outcome.

    A. Don will continue to set the alarm to the sound of ocean waves.

    B. Don will continue to set the alarm to the beeping sound.

    C. Don will continue to set the alarm to the sound of birds chirping.

School Lunch

Reggie almost always brings a sandwich from home to eat for lunch at school. He says he only likes to eat school lunches on days when they offer chicken nuggets. Yesterday, the school lunch option was cheese pizza, so Reggie brought a sandwich to eat. Today, the school is offering chicken nuggets.

Predict the outcome.

    A. Reggie will probably eat cheese pizza for lunch.

    B. Reggie will probably eat a sandwich for lunch.

    C. Reggie will probably eat chicken nuggets for lunch.

Name _____   **Date** _____

Castle Construction

Eva and Jenna wanted to build sandcastles while they played at the beach. For building sandcastles, Eva knew that dry sand does not work as well as wet sand. Dry sand does not stick together like wet sand does. Eva sat closer to the water to build her sandcastle where the sand is wet. Jenna sat farther from the water (where the sand is dry) to build her sandcastle.

Predict the outcome.

    A. Eva's sandcastle will not stick together.

    B. Jenna's sandcastle will not stick together.

    C. Eva and Jenna will build a sandcastle together.

Ankle Twister

Suzie was excited to go to school on Thursday. During P.E., the fourth and fifth graders were going to start playing softball. Her class was going to play against Mr. Copper's class at the end of the school day. While Suzie was playing during morning recess, she tripped over a friend's backpack, spraining her ankle. It hurt so much that she couldn't even walk on it.

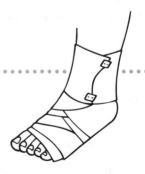

Predict the outcome.

    A. Suzie will never trip over anything again.

    B. Suzie will play in the softball game.

    C. Suzie will not play in the softball game.

Juice It Up

Mr. and Mrs. Barnett got a juicer as an anniversary gift. It can make juice from fruits and vegetables. The directions said to remove the seeds from fruits before using. Mr. Barnett cut up three red apples and three green apples. He cut all the seeds out, and then Mrs. Barnett put the apple pieces into the juicer.

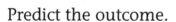

Predict the outcome.

    A. Apple juice will come out of the juicer.

    B. Mr. and Mrs. Barnett will try yellow apples next.

    C. The juicer will not work correctly.

Zoo Map

A new exhibit was being opened at the zoo. A glass tunnel had been added into the penguin area. People could stand in the tunnel and watch penguins swim all around them. Sarah couldn't wait to go to the zoo and see the new penguin exhibit. When Sarah got to the zoo, she located a zoo map. The bird section was laid out in a straight path. The birds that could fly were at the start of the path. Parrots were between the eagles and the ducks. The penguins were at the very end of the bird section. Other flightless birds like the emu and ostrich were located between the ducks and the penguins.

Predict the outcome.

    A. Sarah will see emus before she sees eagles.

    B. Penguins will be the only birds Sarah sees that can swim.

    C. Sarah will see parrots before she sees penguins.

Name _____ **Date** _____

A Cold Lesson

David went snowboarding with his family. He wore snow pants, a snow jacket, and a beanie, but he forgot to bring his gloves. David is a beginning snowboarder. His parents signed him up for a snowboarding lesson so that he could learn. David fell down a lot during his lesson.

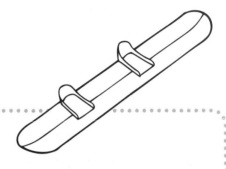

Predict the outcome.

    A. David's hands will get cold.
    B. David will never fall once he learns how to snowboard.
    C. David will not learn how to snowboard.

Time to Eat

Marco woke up very late this morning. He only had enough time to both get dressed and brush his teeth before he had to leave for school. He did not have time to eat breakfast or to pack a lunch. Marco was very hungry at lunchtime. All he ate was a granola bar he found in his backpack. When Marco came home from school, he walked straight to the refrigerator.

Predict the outcome.

    A. Marco will eat food from the refrigerator.
    B. Marco will buy food from a restaurant.
    C. Marco will wait until dinner to eat.

Name _____ **Date** _____

Wet Apples

The teacher asked the class if they thought an apple would sink or float when the apple was placed into a tub of water. At first, Clara thought an apple would sink. Then, she remembered playing a fun game called "bobbing for apples" at a party. In the game, players tried to catch with their teeth one of the apples that was floating in a bucket of water. Clara raised her hand to answer the question.

Predict the outcome.

A. Clara will say that an apple would sink.
B. Clara will say that an apple would float.
C. Clara will say that she doesn't know what the apple will do.

Pop Music

Scarlett likes to listen to pop music every time she cleans. She says the music is upbeat and makes cleaning more fun. Scarlett has a collection of pop music. Today, Scarlett is going to clean her bedroom. She put on her headphones and turned up the volume.

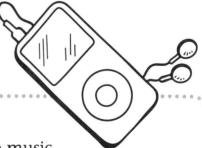

Predict the outcome.

A. Scarlett will fall asleep while listening to pop music.
B. Scarlett will sing along with the pop music.
C. Scarlett will listen to pop music while she cleans.

Name _____ **Date** _____

Learning to Draw

Luke checked out a book from the library called *How to Draw Farm Animals.* Each page showed a different animal and had step-by-step directions on how to draw it. The first few pages showed a horse, a chicken, and a pig. Luke flipped to the cow page. He took out a paper and a pencil and carefully followed each step.

Predict the outcome.

- **A.** Luke will draw a farm.
- **B.** Luke will draw a cow.
- **C.** Luke will read about a cow.

Shadow Tag

Ian likes to play shadow tag. In shadow tag, the person who is "it" doesn't have to touch another person to make them "it." All they need to do is step on the other person's shadow. To be safe, people can run into shady areas so their own shadows cannot be seen. Isabella doesn't like to play tag. She told Ian she will only play shadow tag at twelve noon.

Predict the outcome.

- **A.** Ian and Isabella's shadow tag game will not work because everyone's shadow will be too short.
- **B.** It will be easy for the person who is "it" to tag others because everyone will have a very long shadow.
- **C.** Ian will enjoy playing shadow tag at noon with Isabella because her shadow will be twice as long as his.

Name _____ **Date** _____

The **main idea** of your story is what it is mostly about. Often, a title gives you a hint about the main idea. If you were seeing a movie called *The Beast from the Blue Lagoon*, you wouldn't expect the movie to be about how to cook carrots.

How Terrific Is Your Title?

Below, write five sentences. In your sentences, make up a book or movie title. Your title should state, or at least hint at, your main idea. Then tell what your book or movie will be about. Your titles and sentences can be serious or silly, but all your sentences must follow the sentence structure in the example.

Example:

One day, I will write a book called <u>My Home Planet</u>, and it will be about Jupiter. In addition, it will have a part about the day the aliens from Earth flew by in a spaceship.

Make sure you remember to underline your book and movie titles!

1. One day, I will write a book called _____,
   and it will be about _____. In addition,
   _____.

2. _____

   _____

   _____

3. _____

   _____

   _____

4. _____

   _____

   _____

5. _____

   _____

   _____

Name _____ **Date** _____

Under the Sea

Imagine you are part of the "New Frontier." You live in an underwater city. Your school has been paired with a "topside" school that is on land. You have been asked to write one or two paragraphs for a "topside" student about what students in your class do for fun at recess.

In the first sentences, begin by introducing yourself and describing where your school is located. (What ocean will you pick?) Then, you must focus on the **main idea**: one game that you play at recess or a fun activity you participate in at recess.

Your game can be one you make up, or it can be a popular "topside" game (like basketball, baseball, or hopscotch) that has been changed so that it can be played underwater. When you write, think about the game rules and objectives. Also, consider what you might wear when you play your game, how things move differently under the water, and what equipment you will use.

Remember! Stick to just one game or activity!

_____

_____

_____

_____

_____

_____

_____

_____

_____

Name _____ **Date** _____

An *autobiography* is a book about a person written by that person. In an autobiography, the author describes facts about his or her life, actions, and feelings.

Dog Days

An autobiography is typically written in the *first-person point of view*. This means the author will use such words as **I**, **me**, **we**, and **us** to tell the story.

You are going to write an autobiography, but it will likely be unlike any autobiography you have written before. You will need to imagine that you are a pet! You can be a cat, a dog, or any other kind of pet you can think of.

Write a paragraph or two in which you describe what you look like, what happens to you, how you feel, how you are treated, and an adventure you have had.

Remember to keep your autobiography in the first-person point of view.

_____

_____

_____

_____

_____

_____

_____

_____

_____

_____

_____

Name _____ **Date** _____

Imagine you are a newspaper reporter. You write for an online newspaper, and the picture below is part of your story. Think of a caption that can go underneath the picture. The caption should be short and sum up the action. The caption should fit with the **main idea** of the story.

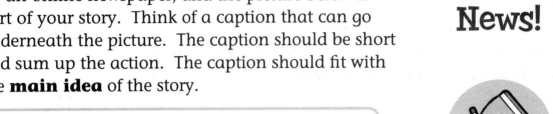

_____

_____

Now, write a paragraph in which you explain more about what is going on in the picture. Use your imagination to fill in details about **where**, **when**, **what**, **why**, and **how**.

_____

_____

_____

_____

_____

_____

_____

_____

Name _____   **Date** _____

Think about the 50 states that make up the United States. They all have similarities as well as differences.

Write five sentences below. In each sentence, compare and contrast any two states by explaining how they are *similar* and how they are *different*.

50 Nifty States

Example:

Washington and Oregon are similar because they both border the Pacific Ocean, but Washington is closer than Oregon to the Canadian border.

Remember to put a comma before the word *but*!

1. _____ and _____ are similar because they both

   _____, but _____

   _____.

2. _____

   _____

   _____

3. _____

   _____

   _____

4. _____

   _____

   _____

5. _____

   _____

   _____

Name _____ **Date** _____

Think of a person. It can be someone famous or someone sitting right next to you. Now think of <u>twenty</u> details about that person. Write them down. **Start with the most general** (*example: she is alive; she is no longer living*) and **end with the most specific** (*example: his initials are RLS; his first name is Robert*).

Let's Get Specific

1. _____
2. _____
3. _____
4. _____
5. _____
6. _____
7. _____
8. _____
9. _____
10. _____
11. _____
12. _____
13. _____
14. _____
15. _____
16. _____
17. _____
18. _____
19. _____
20. _____

Read your details to your classmates, or share them in a small group. Which of your classmates was first able to figure out who you were describing? _____

Name _____   **Date** _____

Haiku is a traditional form of Japanese poetry. Haiku poems often deal with something in nature. In an English form of haiku, the poem has three lines. The first and last lines have five syllables each. The middle line has seven syllables.

Do You Haiku?

You are going to write two haiku poems. The first one will be a "What Am I?" haiku. In this poem, you will give details about an animal without naming it.

What Am I?

Example:

Beautiful green skin (5 syllables)
Powerful legs to jump with (7 syllables)
My small world is wet (5 syllables)

Could you guess that this poem is about a frog?

_____

_____

_____

The second poem will be a "nature" haiku. It will be about a season or something in nature.

Nature

Example:

Diamonds from the sky (5 syllables)
White blanket over the ground (7 syllables)
Flowers in deep sleep (5 syllables)

This haiku poem is about snow falling in winter.

_____

_____

_____

When you have finished, staple a copy of everyone's poems together to make a book. Could your classmates guess what you were writing about?

Name _____ **Date** _____

Toy Sale!
50% Off!

Look
Closer

Sometimes, we need to look closer at a picture to notice all of the details. Look carefully at the picture above for as many details as you can. Write four details from the picture in the spaces below.

1. _____

2. _____

3. _____

4. _____

Now, use your details to write a paragraph about what you think is happening in this picture. First, talk about the "big picture," and then focus on the details.

_____

_____

_____

_____

_____

_____

_____

_____

_____

Name _____   **Date** _____

Often, the author of a story does not tell you everything about a character. To learn more about a character, you sometimes have to rely on clues from the environment, such as the way the character acts or what he or she says.

What Did You Say?

Think of four different professions (jobs). Then, write a sentence about each profession. Don't name the profession in your sentence, but include some words the person might say as well as an appropriate action.

Example:

As Nolan put the finishing touches on the plans, he said, "This building is going to have 100 floors." (architect)

Remember to capitalize the first word in the quotation marks.

1. As _____

_____ said, "_____

_____."

2. _____

_____

_____

3. _____

_____

_____

4. _____

_____

_____

Now pass your paper to three of your classmates. Have each of them write what profession they think the sentences are about. Let them know if they are correct or not.

Name _____   **Date** _____

Imagine that you are a coin. Write a paragraph sharing your inner thoughts. Make it sound as if you are on an amazing journey. Your journey can be fun, exciting, or even dangerous, but *don't reveal that you are a coin until the very last line!* Try to keep your true identity a secret until the end of your story.

The Amazing Journey!

Example **beginning** sentences:

It's so crowded and dark in here.

Help, I'm falling!

I must have rolled twenty feet down the sidewalk.

Example **ending** sentences:

A dime may be worth more, but I'm glad I'm just a penny.

At least this time I ended up in a piggy bank instead of being tossed into a wishing well!

_____

_____

_____

_____

_____

_____

_____

_____

_____

Read your paragraph out loud to a friend or to the entire class. Put a lot of emotion into your voice. How believable are you as a coin? Would someone hearing your paragraph for the first time be surprised at the end by your true identity?

Name _____   **Date** _____

Look at the pictures below. You are not told how old the children are in the pictures, but most likely, you can tell. For each picture, write a paragraph in which you start by sharing what grade you think the children are in as well as their approximate ages. Next, explain what details in the pictures helped you come to your conclusions. Were there any clues that were particularly helpful? Any that weren't helpful at all?

Classroom Clues

_____
_____
_____
_____
_____
_____
_____
_____

_____
_____
_____
_____
_____
_____
_____
_____

Name _____ **Date** _____

Two hard words to read are *colossal* and *miniscule*.

When something is *colossal*, it is huge or gigantic.

When something is *miniscule*, it is very small.

Imagine you are teaching someone what these two hard words mean. Without stating their definitions, write three sentences each (six in all) using each word.

Two of the sentences have been started for you.

Building Your Vocabulary

1. I made a *colossal* mistake when I _____

_____

2. _____

_____

_____

3. _____

_____

4. The recipe called for a *miniscule* amount of hot pepper, but unfortunately

_____

5. _____

_____

6. _____

_____

Do you think someone could figure out what *colossal* and *miniscule* mean after reading your sentences? How?

_____

_____

_____

Name _____ **Date** _____

Speak Your Mind

A **fact** is a thing that has happened. A fact is true.

An **opinion** is what you think.

What type of milk does your school offer? Some schools provide regular and chocolate milk. Other schools provide low-fat and non-fat milk, too. Some people think schools should not offer chocolate milk or any milk with a higher fat content. What do you think? Why?

Construct a paragraph using facts and opinions to support your answer.

Write a paragraph in which your **first** sentence starts out like this:

It is a fact that my school offers _____ *milk.*

Your **second** sentence starts out like this:

It is my opinion that _____

_____

Sentences **three** and **four** (more if you want) should tell *why* you think so. Give reasons why your opinion is a good one!

I believe this because _____

_____

_____

_____

The **last** sentence should start out like this:

In conclusion, I feel schools across the nation should _____

_____

_____

On a separate piece of paper, combine the sentences from above to form a complete paragraph supporting your opinion.

Name _____ **Date** _____

Write a dialogue between two people discussing sports. In your dialogue, have each person say at least one **fact** and one **opinion** about a sport.

Sports Talk

When you write, pick your own character names.

Remember to put a colon after the name of the person speaking!

Example:

Dora: The most interesting sport to watch is volleyball. *(opinion)*

Adam: That's your opinion, and I don't agree. I think soccer is more exciting to watch. *(opinion)*

Dora: That's your opinion. Watching soccer makes me want to take a nap. *(opinion)*

Adam: What? It is a fact that a soccer field is bigger than a volleyball court. *(fact)*

Dora: True, but it is also a fact that some volleyball tournaments take place on the beach. *(fact)*

_____

_____

_____

_____

_____

_____

_____

_____

Pick two classmates to read your dialogue to the class. Have the class identify which of your sentences are facts and which are opinions.

Name _____ **Date** _____

Is the story in the box below true? Write a paragraph in which you discuss whether or not this story is factual, and why. Make sure you support your answer with **facts**.

Believe It or Not?

Your paragraph should include transition words (such as *additionally* and *furthermore*), and should include a strong concluding sentence. Your final sentence should remind the reader your **opinion** about how true this story is. You may finish the final sentence below or you can make up a completely new one.

> *The Statue of Liberty is in California. It is a statue of a gold miner. It is located on Angel Island. The statue was a gift from Brazil. Brazil is a country in Europe. People in Brazil speak Russian, and there is a poem on the Statue of Liberty in Russian. One line from the poem says, "Give me your rich and healthy." The statue is about twenty feet tall. It is made of solid steel, so no one can go inside of it.*

_____

_____

_____

_____

_____

_____

_____

_____

It is my opinion that this story is _____

_____

_____

As part of a scientific experiment, you are going to be left alone on a tropical island for six months. You are going to be allowed to take with you only three things. The three objects must fit into a small backpack. Below, list the three things you will bring to help you survive, and explain why you chose each item.

Survival Supplies

Item 1: _____ **Why?** _____

Item 2: _____ **Why?** _____

Item 3: _____ **Why?** _____

Now, write a paragraph describing what you will bring and why. The paragraph has been started for you.

If I were left on a tropical island for six months, it is a fact that the

three items I would fit into my backpack would be _____ **,**

_____ **, and** _____ **. It is my opinion that there**

can be no better items than these because _____

_____

_____

_____

_____

_____

_____

Name _____ **Date** _____

Finding Cause and Effect

Read this sentence:

When I heard that a thirteen-foot boa constrictor had escaped from the zoo, I looked under my bed before I went to sleep.

When I heard that a thirteen-foot boa constrictor had escaped from the zoo is the **cause**. It is **why** it happened.

I looked under my bed before I went to sleep is the **effect**. It is **what** happened.

Practice writing the part of the sentence that is the **cause**.

1. When _____, I decided I wasn't hungry.

2. _____, so I hid the gold inside under a floorboard in my closet.

Practice writing the part of the sentence that is the **effect**.

1. After seeing the spaceship land in the back yard, _____

_____.

2. When I heard that the volcano might erupt, _____

_____.

Now try one on your own. Make sure your sentence has both a cause and an effect. <u>Underline</u> the cause. (Circle) the effect.

_____

_____

_____

_____

_____

Name _____ **Date** _____

Living without Lines

Think about how many times each day you stand in a line. Now imagine a society in which no one stands in lines. Write a paragraph or two in which you first explain what type of society you live in. Then describe one or two scenes in which no one stands in a line. These scenes may be at a movie theater, in the cafeteria, at a ball game, or anywhere you like. What is it like? How do you feel? Your paragraph can be realistic, imaginative, or funny.

End your paragraph with a strong concluding sentence. You may finish the one below or you can make up a completely new one.

_____

_____

_____

_____

_____

_____

_____

_____

_____

After describing what a society would be like without lines, it is my

conclusion that _____

_____

_____

Fables are short stories with a moral at the end. A moral is a brief lesson about what is right. Most likely, you are familiar with the fable about the tortoise and the hare. The tortoise bets the hare that he can beat the hare in a race. The hare is faster, but because he is overconfident, he takes a nap during the race. The tortoise ends up winning, and so the moral is, "Slow and steady wins the race."

Twisted Fables

What if the race had different results, and the hare won? Would the story have the same effect? Would it have the same moral? No, it would not!

Now it's time for you to *rewrite* a fable! It can be the fable about the tortoise and the hare, or a different one with which you are already familiar. After you create your *new* version of the fable, be sure to include a moral at the end, sharing the lesson of your story.

_____

_____

_____

_____

_____

_____

_____

_____

_____

_____

Moral: _____

Name _____ **Date** _____

The Door

Write a story about a boy or girl who takes a trip to visit his or her great aunt. Describe how, while exploring the great aunt's house, the child discovers a small locked door. When the boy or girl asks their great aunt about the door, the great aunt gets upset and says something like, "Don't ever open that door!" Of course they don't listen, so tell what happens when the boy or girl opens the door!

Your story can be fantastic, realistic, or silly. Use your imagination and have fun!

_____

_____

_____

_____

_____

_____

_____

_____

_____

_____

_____

_____

_____

_____

Name _____ **Date** _____

One afternoon, an alien from Mars comes to visit you. You tell the alien that you have an extra bike and that the two of you can ride to the park. When you get to the bike, the alien stares at it for a few seconds, then flips it upside down and starts to lick the tires! Next, the alien lifts the bike up over its head and runs backwards with it!

The Alien and the Bicycle

You try to explain to the alien the correct way to ride a bike, but it gets embarrassed and hides behind a tree. Unable to get the alien to cooperate, you decide to leave behind written instructions so that it can practice without anyone watching.

Think about all the steps that go into riding a bike. Break down the process into very small steps for the alien. Write down the steps in order. Make sure to use proper sequencing words such as **first**, **second**, **then**, **next**, **after**, and **finally**.

If you want, you can include small drawings.

_____

_____

_____

_____

_____

_____

_____

_____

_____

_____

Name _____ **Date** _____

Imagine you arrive home after a two-week vacation, and animals have overrun your entire house. Everywhere you look, you see animals. Pets from the neighborhood are taking naps on your couch; animals from the forest are rummaging through your kitchen cupboards. You even see some escaped animals from the zoo running in circles in your living room. You have a big problem on your hands!

Animal House

Write a story explaining what animals are in your house, how they got inside, why they've taken over, and most importantly, how you're going to solve the problem. Your solution should include a detailed explanation *including what steps you will take, and in what order*. What will you do first? Second? Then what? Be creative!

_____

_____

_____

_____

_____

_____

_____

_____

_____

_____

_____

_____

_____

_____

_____

Name _____ **Date** _____

When you write, these words help the reader know when things happened:

> **first**, **second**, **third**, **before**, **previously**, **then**, **next**, **finally**, **after**

River Ramble

Use at least *seven* of these words when you make up a story about riding on a raft or a canoe down a river. Choose any river you like, such as the Nile, the Amazon, or the Mississippi. Underline the words you use from the list.

Example:

<u>After</u> I went down the Nile River on the back of a crocodile, I decided my <u>next</u> trip would be to . . .

_____

_____

_____

_____

_____

_____

_____

_____

_____

_____

_____

_____

Name _____ **Date** _____

Look at the pictures. Think about what happened first, second, third, and last. Are the pictures in the correct order? Write a **1**, **2**, **3**, or **4** under each picture to show the correct order. Next, use these pictures to create a story, and write a paragraph explaining what happened.

Out of Order

_____

_____

_____

_____

_____

_____

_____

_____

_____

_____

Name _____ **Date** _____

When writing, the setting of your story can be a very powerful tool. Below, write three short paragraphs that occur in three different settings. In one paragraph, write as if you are in a place *below* the ground. In another paragraph, you are in a place *on* the ground. In yet another paragraph, you are in a place *above* the ground.

Where AM I?

Write your paragraphs in any order. Do not reveal whether you are below, on, or above the ground! Make your reader figure it out by your descriptions and your actions.

Location 1: _____

_____

_____

_____

_____

Location 2: _____

_____

_____

_____

_____

Location 3: _____

_____

_____

_____

Read each of your paragraphs to a classmate. Could they guess where you were located? Which location was the most difficult for them to figure out?

_____

_____

Name _____ **Date** _____

A cookie crime has been committed! Someone has taken all the cookies out of the cookie jar, and Grandma isn't too happy about it. After collecting clues and talking to witnesses, Grandma has narrowed down her suspect list to just three animals: Clarissa the Cow, Charles the Chicken, and Pete the Pig. It's now up to you to help Grandma find the true cookie criminal. Looking at the three suspects below, who do you think is guilty? Write a paragraph identifying who you believe took the cookies, and explain how you came to this conclusion. Provide at least **five** reasons for your conclusion.

Whodunnit?

Clarissa the Cow

Charles the Chicken

Pete the Pig

_____

_____

_____

_____

_____

_____

_____

_____

_____

_____

_____

Name _____ **Date** _____

Some people treat their pets like their babies. Sometimes if you close your eyes and listen to a person talking to their pet, you may be unsure if they are talking to an animal or to a real human baby!

Talking To Yourself

Write a paragraph in which you have a one-sided dialogue with a pet or human baby, but don't reveal whom you are talking to. Make the reader **infer** whom you are talking to! Try to be as *vague* as possible, yet make it sound as if you are really talking. When you are done, read your paragraph to a few classmates. Were they able to figure out whether you were talking to an animal or a human?

Example:

"Oh, you cute little thing. Let me brush your hair."

_____

_____

_____

_____

_____

_____

_____

_____

_____

_____

_____

_____

_____

_____

Name _____ **Date** _____

In the pictures below, you are not told what is going to happen next, but you can come up with some good ideas!

Write down a sentence or two in which you describe the scene. Then tell what is going to happen *next*.

Use your imagination when you write your sentences, and try your best to entertain the reader!

What Happens Next?

_____
_____
_____
_____
_____
_____
_____
_____

_____
_____
_____
_____
_____
_____
_____

Name _____ **Date** _____

Children's stories often have wild and fun plots. Sometimes, food falls from the sky. Other times, buses can fly. Imagine that you are a children's author who is writing a picture book. The main idea is that a child wants their hair to grow faster. The child somehow gets a bottle of "Miracle Hair Grow," but when the bottle is opened, something surprising happens! What happens? Will the streets be blocked with hair? Will the hair save someone? It is all up to you! Have fun with your imagination!

A Hairy Situation

Use the information below to help guide your writing.

First Paragraph: Who is the child? What does he or she want? How is the bottle found?

Second Paragraph: What happens when the hair won't stop growing?

Third Paragraph: How is the problem solved?

_____

_____

_____

_____

_____

_____

_____

_____

_____

_____

_____

Name _____ **Date** _____

Imagine you were just hired to be the new weather reporter for your local radio station. It's your first day, and you are broadcasting your weather prediction over the radio. Write down what you might say.

First Day on the Job

First, greet your listeners and identify yourself and the station. Then report the current weather (temperature, wind speed, sky cover, and precipitation*). Next, make up a forecast for the next day. Your forecast should be for something very unusual—perhaps a blizzard, heat wave, tornado, or hurricane. Tell people what they should do to prepare.

Conclude your broadcast by signing off. You can use the example below, add to it, or make up a completely new one.

The beginning and the end of your weather report have been started for you. Use additional paper if necessary.

Good evening, ladies and gentlemen, my name is _____,

and you're listening to _____.

_____

_____

_____

_____

_____

_____

_____

Rain or shine, I'll be here tomorrow. This is _____

signing off. Thanks for listening. _____

   * *Precipitation is rain, sleet, snow, or hail.*

Common Core State Standards Correlations

Each activity in *Instant Reading Comprehension Practice* meets one or more of the following Common Core State Standards (© Copyright 2010. National Governors Association Center for Best Practices and Council of Chief State School Officers. All rights reserved.). For more information about the Common Core State Standards, go to *http://www.corestandards.org* or visit *http://www.teachercreated.com/standards*.

Reading: Literature	
Key Ideas and Details	**Pages**
ELA-Literacy.RL.4.1 Refer to details and examples in a text when explaining what the text says explicitly and when drawing inferences from the text.	21–31, 33–35, 81–95
ELA-Literacy.RL.4.2 Determine a theme of a story, drama, or poem from details in the text; summarize the text.	6–15, 17, 19–20
ELA-Literacy.RL.4.3 Describe in depth a character, setting, or event in a story or drama, drawing on specific details in the text (e.g., a character's thoughts, words, or actions).	66–80, 96–110
Craft and Structure	**Pages**
ELA-Literacy.RL.4.4 Determine the meaning of words and phrases as they are used in a text, including those that allude to significant characters found in mythology (e.g., Herculean).	36–50
Range of Reading and Level of Text Complexity	**Pages**
ELA-Literacy.RL.4.10 By the end of the year, read and comprehend literature, including stories, dramas, and poetry, in the grades 4–5 text complexity band proficiently, with scaffolding as needed at the high end of the range.	6–15, 17, 19–31, 33–110
Reading: Informational Text	
Key Ideas and Details	**Pages**
ELA-Literacy.RI.4.1 Refer to details and examples in a text when explaining what the text says explicitly and when drawing inferences from the text.	21, 23, 26, 29, 31–35, 83, 86, 89, 95
ELA-Literacy.RI.4.2 Determine the main idea of a text and explain how it is supported by key details; summarize the text.	8, 10–12, 14–18
ELA-Literacy.RI.4.3 Explain events, procedures, ideas, or concepts in a historical, scientific, or technical text, including what happened and why, based on specific information in the text.	21, 23, 26, 29, 31–32, 35, 57, 59, 64, 83, 86, 89, 95, 98–99, 104
Craft and Structure	**Pages**
ELA-Literacy.RI.4.4 Determine the meaning of general academic and domain-specific words or phrases in a text relevant to a *grade 4 topic or subject area*.	43
ELA-Literacy.RI.4.5 Describe the overall structure (e.g., chronology, comparison, cause/effect, problem/solution) of events, ideas, concepts, or information in a text or part of a text.	57, 59, 64, 70
Integration of Knowledge and Ideas	**Pages**
ELA-Literacy.RI.4.8 Explain how an author uses reasons and evidence to support particular points in a text.	57, 59, 64

Range of Reading and Level of Text Complexity	Pages
ELA-Literacy.RI.4.10 By the end of year, read and comprehend informational texts, including history/social studies, science, and technical texts, in the grades 4–5 text complexity band proficiently, with scaffolding as needed at the high end of the range.	8, 10–12, 14–18, 21, 23, 26, 29, 31–35, 43, 51–55, 57, 59, 64, 70, 83, 86, 89, 95, 98–99, 104

Reading: Foundational Skills

Phonics and Word Recognition	Pages
ELA-Literacy.RF.4.3 Know and apply grade-level phonics and word analysis skills in decoding words.	6–110

Fluency	Pages
ELA-Literacy.RF.4.4 Read with sufficient accuracy and fluency to support comprehension.	6–110

Writing

Text Type and Purposes	Pages
ELA-Literacy.W.4.1 Write opinion pieces on topics or texts, supporting a point of view with reasons and information.	123–126
ELA-Literacy.W.4.2 Write informative/explanatory texts to examine a topic and convey ideas and information clearly.	114–116, 118–119, 121–122, 128, 131–132, 134, 138
ELA-Literacy.W.4.3 Write narratives to develop real or imagined experiences or events using effective technique, descriptive details, and clear event sequences.	111–114, 118, 120, 126–140

Production and Distribution of Writing	Pages
ELA-Literacy.W.4.4 Produce clear and coherent writing in which the development and organization are appropriate to task, purpose, and audience. (Grade-specific expectations for writing types are defined in standards 1–3.)	111–140
ELA-Literacy.W.4.5 With guidance and support from peers and adults, develop and strengthen writing as needed by planning, revising, and editing. (Editing for conventions should demonstrate command of Language standards 1–3 up to and including grade 4 here.)	111–140

Range of Writing	Pages
ELA-Literacy.W.4.10 Write routinely over extended time frames (time for research, reflection, and revision) and shorter time frames (a single sitting or a day or two) for a range of discipline-specific tasks, purposes, and audiences.	111–140

Answer Key

Finding Main Ideas

Page 6
Be Careful What
  You Wish For: A
Surprising Visit: B

Page 7
A Day for Dad: C
Night Talking: A

Page 8
Dress-Up Drama: C
Island Living: B

Page 9
Debbie's Diner: A
Too Short!: C

Page 10
Street Ball: C
Jumping Over
  Obstacles: B

Page 11
Camera Man: A
Water Pups: B

Page 12
Super Swimmers: A
Bike Dreams: B

Page 13
Up and Away: C
Portrait Problems: A

Page 14
Turtle Tales: A
Different Answers: C

Page 15
Bad Day at the Beach: B
Hang Up: B

Page 16
Cool Shades: C
Presidential Prerequisites: C

Page 17
Meg the Mower: A
Blue-Blooded: B

Page 18
The Escape of
  Fu Manchu: B
Tasty Trees: C

Page 19
Tryout Jitters: C
Going Green: B

Page 20
Hatching Memories: A
No Vote from Mom?: A

Noting Details

Page 21
After-School Activities: B
Balancing Meals: A

Page 22
Support Our School: A
Healthy Habits: C

Page 23
Standing Room Only: B
Surviving the Cold: A

Page 24
Summer Vacation: C
Secret Savings: C

Page 25
Dancing Raisins: A
Grandma's Gift: A

Page 26
Talented Twins: A
Long-Distance Flyer: C

Page 27
Mountain Bike: B
Brain Freeze: B

Page 28
Grape Idea!: C
Mystery Baby: C

Page 29
Best Field Trip Ever!: B
Tremendous Tower: C

Page 30
Unexpected Workout: A
Giving Thanks: B

Page 31
Wolves of the Sea: C
Movie Mistakes: B

Page 32
Small Friends: A
Mighty Maine: A

Page 33
Safe Swimming: B
Which One Are You?: A

Page 34
Muy Delicioso: A
Forever Stamp: A

Page 35
Dance Partners: C
Caring Crabs: B

Using Context Clues

Page 36
Super Scholar: C
Pobody Is Nerfect: A

Page 37
Brotherly Love?: C
Tastes Like Sofa: B

Page 38
Making the Family Fit: B
Nice Day for a Stroll: A

Page 39
Sweet Science: A
Pick a Prize: B

Page 40
Ready for Winter: C
A Wacky Habit: C

Page 41
Reaching the Summit: B
Grandma's Stories: A

Page 42
Sweet Treats: A
Magical Party: C

Page 43
Stars and Stripes: B
Discovered Talent: C

Page 44
Good Science: B
Mom's New Recipe: A

Page 45
Foliage Fashion: C
A Little Research: A

Page 46
Finding the Area: B
Missing Recess: A

Page 47
Spelling Pride: A
Flying High: C

Page 48
Every Drop Counts: C
Watch Closely!: B

Page 49
Daily Warm-Up: B
Book Club: C

Page 50
Little Stars: A
Mind Your Manners: B

Identifying Facts and Opinions

Page 51
City Living: A, B
Beach Days: A, C
Chocolate Milk: A, C
Water Sports: B, C
Air Jordan: A, C
Name That Dog: A, B

Page 52
Now I Know My ABCs: A, B
Red, White, and Blue: A, C
Some Pig!: B, C
Bright Ideas: A, C
A Day to Celebrate: A, B
February: A, C

Page 53
Creepy, Crawly,
  and Amazing: B, C
Roses Are Red . . .
  and White: A, C
Picture Pages: A, C
Morning Ride: A, B
Out of This World: B, C
Sleepy Solutions: B, C

Page 54
Worldly Words: A, B
Typing Trouble: B, C
Soccer or Football?: B, C
Month by Month: A, B
Add It Up: A, C
Big Cats: B, C

Page 55
Same or Opposite?: A, B
Bike Smart: A, B
Turkey Day: B, C
Presidential Palace: A, C
Not Real Glass: A, C
Borrowing Books: A, B

Finding Cause and Effect

Page 56
Two-Alarm Morning: B
Lost and Found: A
Hot Walk: C

Page 57
Family Wardrobe: B
Making Green: C
Wild Eyes: A

Page 58
Young Scientists: C
RSVP: A
Homework Helper: C

Page 59
Clean and Shout: B
Perilous Plunge: C
Finding a Home for the
    President: B

Page 60
Squeaky Steps: B
Out of the Picture: A
Freeze Tag: A

Page 61
Swinging by
    the Hospital: A
Candle Complications: C
Solve the Riddle: B

Page 62
Late-Night Gaming: A
One More Canary: B
Water Hazard: C

Page 63
No Peeking!: B
Insert Another Quarter: B
Hard-Earned Money: A

Page 64
Koala (Not) Bears: C
Canned-Vegetable
    Garden: B
Change of Plans: A

Page 65
Morning Visitor: C
Two Right Answers?: A
Way Too Heavy: C

Sequencing

Page 66
Morning Routine: A
Good Citizen: C

Page 67
Color Change: B
Helping Hands: B

Page 68
Fall Colors: C
Sailing East: C

Page 69
Candy Math: A
Alphabet Assessment: A

Page 70
Summer Fun: B
Simple Sandwich: C

Page 71
Party Planner: A
Recess Romp: B

Page 72
A Sinking Feeling: B
Food List: A

Page 73
Use Your Head: C
A Gift for Mom: C

Page 74
It's a Riddle: A
Pizza Delivery: B

Page 75
Beginner's Luck: B
Goodbye, Flame: C

Page 76
Lost in the Zoo: A
Math Minded: B

Page 77
An Important Tail: B
Barking Loudly: C

Page 78
Snow Friend: B
Toddler Television: C

Page 79
Where Did I Put That?: A
Seasonal Spirit: A

Page 80
"Eggciting" Science: C
Campaign Trail: A

Making Inferences

Page 81
Under Pressure: A
Road Trip: C

Page 82
Feeling like a
    New Man: B
Island Dream: A

Page 83
Safe Swimmer: B
Ask an Engineer: A

Page 84
Man in Black . . .
    and White: C
Cup of Pellets: B

Page 85
Familiar Friends: A
Unwelcome Surprise: C

Page 86
In Costume: C
Snow Scenes: B

Page 87
Book Batteries: A
Tomato Twins: B

Page 88
A Little Extra Help: A
Digging Up Trouble: B

Page 89
Fruit Exchange: C
Pikes Peak: C

Page 90
Easy Money: A
Morning Exercise: A

Page 91
No Hands: C
All Shook Up: B

Page 92
Lights Out: A
Foggy Surprise: C

Page 93
Mouse Madness: C
Quarter Races: B

Page 94
A Fancy Invitation: B
Well-Prepared: A

Page 95
Delayed Dinner: C
Two-Headed Snake: B

Predicting Outcomes

Page 96
Pool Party: A
Dollar Scoops: C

Page 97
Pay to Play: C
Blue Glue: B

Page 98
No Recipe Required: A
Tilted Axis: B

Page 99
Animal Acrobatics: B
Peanuts and Sprinkles: A

Page 100
Rover: C
Family Bowl: C

Page 101
April Showers: C
Planetary Positions: B

Page 102
Candles on the Cake: B
Clean-O: A

Page 103
For Emergency
    Use Only: A
Costume Party: B

Page 104
Cans for Cash: C
"Bloodshot" Eyes: A

Page 105
Morning Beeps: B
School Lunch: C

Page 106
Castle Construction: B
Ankle Twister: C

Page 107
Juice It Up: A
Zoo Map: C

Page 108
A Cold Lesson: A
Time to Eat: A

Page 109
Wet Apples: B
Pop Music: C

Page 110
Learning to Draw: B
Shadow Tag: A